Bernard Baruch

PORTRAIT OF A CITIZEN

Bernard Baruch

PORTRAIT OF A CITIZEN

W. L. White

HARCOURT, BRACE AND COMPANY
NEW YORK

COPYRIGHT, 1950, BY
W. L. WHITE

first edition

PRINTED IN THE UNITED STATES OF AMERICA

Contents

PART ONE

Baruch and Wall Street
(1870-1912)

IT IS JUST POSSIBLE THAT ISAAC RODRI-
quez Marques had been a pirate. At any rate his
great-great-great-great-great-grandson, Bernard Mannes
Baruch, likes elfishly to hope so. But after Isaac Marques arrived in New York in 1696 from the West
Indies, his ships, sailing a triangular course between
Africa, the West Indies and these British North American colonies, kept piously to the rum, molasses, ivory
and slave trade.

We know this because New York was then in the
grip of a reform administration, the Earl of Bellamont
having been sent as the colony's Governor by good
King William the Third to stamp out piracy, and
Bernard Baruch's ancestor does not appear on His
Excellency's record books as having been either fined
or hanged.

Instead in 1697 Isaac Marques became a "freeman,"
taking the oath on the steps of New York's City Hall
adjacent to the town's pillory, ducking-stool, whipping-
post and kindred social welfare devices which this tur-
bulent colonial village of 3,000, still enclosed in its

wooden wall, considered necessary to orderly government. Certainly Nicholas Roosevelt, a respected sugar
importer who was Alderman of Marques' ward, had
no objection to them.

Two generations later Marques' grandson, Isaac, fled
the town as England's red-coats entered, to join Colonel
van Rensselaer's Fourth Albany County regiment.
After the successful revolution Isaac's son, Samuel,
moved to South Carolina where, two generations later,
his granddaughter married Saling Wolfe, their mar-
riage contract being dated "the 70th year of Independence of the United States, and the [Hebrew]
month of Cheshvan 5606," this union presently being
blessed with a daughter Belle, who became our Bernard
Baruch's mother.

Turning to his father's line we find young Simon
Baruch leaving the little Prussian town of Schwersen
in 1855 to make his way to America where he had
learned English reading American history with a dic-
tionary and had been graduated from the Medical College of Virginia when the Civil War broke out. Before
he had ever lanced a boil he joined the Third South
Carolina Battalion, C.S.A., amputated arms and legs
during Bull Run and Antietam, where he was captured
by the Blue Bellies but soon exchanged. He watched
General Pickett's charge at Gettysburg and was again
captured, the Union Army surgeons giving him not

only a wagon for his patients, but also medical supplies, fresh eggs and even wine.

In those ancient, out-moded days men could fight not only with conviction but with chivalry: the Yankee aggressors interned Dr. Baruch in Fort McHenry, but allowed him to go to dances on his word to return to prison after the waltz orchestra had finished playing "Home, Sweet Home." Later there were furloughs during which he could return to South Carolina to continue courting Belle Wolfe, the girl he left behind him, as the story was later told to little Bernie and their other sons.

On one of these furloughs Mis' Belle had painted the young Confederate Captain's picture. Then came a terrible day when the Captain, now attached to the 13th Mississippi Infantry, was far away trying to hold Yankee General Sherman back from the sea, and another wing of Sherman's army swarmed over Saling Wolfe's plantation, setting fire to everything which was too heavy to steal.

One soldier, in spite of Mis' Belle's screams, was carrying off her portrait of Confederate Captain Baruch, when along came a handsome Yankee captain who beat the soldier with the flat of his sword, returned the painting, and then introduced himself to Mis' Belle as Union Captain Cantine. He was of course a Yankee, but still quite good-looking.

Half a century later, after Mis' Belle had in the end

11

married Captain Baruch, after the family had moved up north, and after little Bernie (born in 1870) was not only grown but in Washington, managing the industry of an entire nation in another of our Republic's wars, a young man came to his busy desk with a letter in his mother's so familiar writing.

"The bearer of this is the son of Captain Cantine. I know," Mis' Belle had written in her old lady's hand, "you will do what you can for him."

Captain Baruch came back from his defeated army to a world where the brick chimneys of the old manors towered over the charred wreckage of their rafters, married Mis' Belle and started life as a country doctor in what the Yankees had left of Camden. South Carolina was no longer a state, but only an occupied federal district with a number instead of a name. At first ex-Confederate soldiers could not vote, and the provisional government was elected by their former field-hands, illiterate ex-slaves guided by the Yankee carpetbaggers of the Unionist military government.

Bernard Mannes Baruch, when the war was only five years distant, knew and felt all this as a child, but his life was largely that of any small boy in any small Southern town, with slight differences. There was no synagogue in Camden, but their mother always insisted that on the Jewish Sabbath they should wear their best clothes, with shoes and stockings. On the following

Christian Sunday, out of respect to their neighbors, the boys still were decently dressed, but might go barefoot.

To eke out the income of a country doctor their mother gave piano lessons but (like the Southern lady she was) always had her breakfast served in bed, as before the war.

Her sons remember both her kindliness and her high dignity. "If I can't find something good to say about someone," she would argue, "I don't say anything." All the boys' quarrels had to be ironed out before they went to bed. "Never let the sun go down upon your anger." Her great pride was her table. "I never want one of my boys to go anywhere in the world and get a better meal than they get at home."

Even as children the other Baruch brothers remember little Bernie's burning curiosity about the world. Nearby ran a branch of the Charlotte, Columbia and Augusta railroad. At train time Bernie would always be sitting on the fence, his bare feet locked around its wooden rails, to watch for the smoke and sparks of that old-fashioned, wood-burning locomotive just before it appeared around the bend, dragging its rattling cars. If the train was late, for what reason? If the cars were half-empty, why? If he could find out all about railroads, some day he might even own this one. Years later he almost did, except that J. P. Morgan was willing to pay slightly more than Bernard Baruch thought it was worth.

Then there was the mansion at Winnsboro, with grandfather Saling Wolfe sitting firm and straight as an arrow in his saddle as he rode over his plantation, looking for the world, his daughter Belle insisted, like an English squire. Near the manor was a warehouse which used to be crammed with food for the field-hands. It was still crammed, for the ex-slaves preferred their wages in corn-meal and sow-belly. In a drawer in that mansion were great wads of Confederate money—tens, twenties—even hundred dollar bills—which the occupying Yankees had not even bothered to steal.

Why was some money valuable, but not this? Then little Bernie heard the story of how this money of the Lost Cause, printed in great quantities and with no gold to back it up, had slowly sunk to nothing. This he never forgot.

Then all the Baruch boys remember one election night when their doctor-father was away, and when, after dark, they heard the approaching shouts of a Negro mob which had been liquored up by the scala-wag Yankee politicians. Now all of Camden, black or white, knew that the Baruch boys were good quail shots. So Belle Baruch handed out to the eldest two boys a pair of single-barrelled shot-guns.

"Let them see the guns," she said, "but don't shoot

unless I say so." The mob stayed out of the Baruch yard.

Those exciting years culminated in the great Hayes-Tilden election, when the South realized that, although the Democrats had fairly won the election, the occupying Northern troops were going to count out Tilden in the South, and Colonel Henry Watterson of the Louisville *Courier-Journal* was roaring for 75,000 volunteers to put Tilden in the White House. But a new Civil War was averted when Republican leaders promised the South that when Hayes got in the White House he would bring home the hated Blue-Coats. He did, and the Yankee carpetbaggers left in their wagon trains. Yet for a while there was still struggle: years later the Baruch boys found in an attic trunk not only his Confederate uniform but some strange and ghostly regalia; their Jewish father, like most young Confederate veterans, had been a Knight of the Ku Klux Klan.

Even before little Bernie was in his teens his two brothers had come to see that he had an almost weird ability to brush aside things which did not matter and quickly get at those which did. If half a dozen boys were together, somehow Bernie was always their leader, his brother Herman remembers, and he adds, "Bernie has said of our father, 'He's the most honest-thinking man I ever knew,' but Bernie is even more so. Constantly he seeks facts. Nowadays he gets others to do the spade work, but he absorbs the results. His mind is like that electronic calculator at Harvard; out comes the answer clearly, quickly and accurately, and yet the machine can't tell you how it was arrived at. And it was always that way."

They sensed this even in little Camden, and although the Baruch family moved to New York when little Bernie was only ten, the boys he had played with weren't surprised when presently they began reading his name in the paper. And when, years later, he would come back to visit, the men of that sleepy little unreconstructed Confederate town would gather around.

"Come on, Bernie," they would urge, "tell us how you licked the Yankees in Wall Street!"

But if the electronic brain can't explain how it gets the answer, at least it has an opinion, and on Bernard Baruch's Wall Street desk for many decades was a picture of his straight-thinking old father with this inscription: "Let unswerving integrity always be your guide," the old man had written. The ink had faded little with the years.

Dr. Simon Baruch moved his family to New York and into a house in the East Sixties and quickly they became at home, although his wife, who had to watch the pennies to feed four boys on the income of a struggling physician, would borrow his rig and come back with it loaded with groceries from Washington Market, where things were not only fresher but a little cheaper.

And presently she found, even in this roaring hustling Yankee metropolis, a chapter of her beloved Daughters of the Confederacy as well as of the D.A.R.

Her son, Bernie, at this period was eleven, somewhat quick-tempered, stubby, fat; the neighborhood gang had dubbed him "Bunch." Possibly because other more unpleasant names were occasionally thrown in, the touchy boy began to take boxing lessons at Wood's gymnasium down on 28th Street, where not only the fat melted away but also his temper. It is easy to take with a friendly grin the robust insults of boyhood if you know that, on a showdown, you can unwrap from its tissue paper an uppercut which will stretch the offender out cold in the gutter.

Small wonder then that he still treasures in his library a gift from his teacher, Katherine Blake, of Public School No. 69, "Awarded to Bernard Baruch for Gentlemanly Deportment and General Excellence," a copy of "Oliver Twist." Also for the record, there lived in a smart new brownstone house on nearby 58th Street, a pretty, black-haired little girl named Annie Griffen (daughter of a prosperous glass merchant), who was beginning to appreciate those sterling qualities of heart and mind, particularly when young Bernie at 14 was able to enter a Freshman class of 600 at C.C.N.Y. (his mother feared to let so young a child go to distant Yale) and survive as one of 60 who stood the gaff to graduate.

17

Yet he had one trait which alone could have saved him from being an obnoxious model boy. This was his love of gambling; if it can be strictly called that, for with his remarkable memory, he never had need to falter, to wonder if the trey of clubs had been played; young Bernie Baruch always knew. With this asset he was first spectacularly successful at penny ante, a game forbidden by his worried father. Then he discovered that at John Daley's lavish gambling hell a poor boy, eager to get on in the world, could buy a simple white chip for as little as 50 cents. He had, one night, raised this modest investment to $2 when a familiar shadow fell over his shoulder. The old doctor was standing straight as an arrow.

"Son," he said, and his calm was devastating, "when you are ready, we will go home."

In college young Baruch listened intently while George R. Newcomb, his professor of economics, drummed into his classes the elementary idea that when prices go too high, production increases and consumption falls off, thus pulling them downward. Whereas if prices fall too low, the balance is restored when production dwindles and people begin buying more. This Law of Supply and Demand, which New Deal economists later felt was tediously simple, has never bored Bernard Baruch, for the single reason that through the passing decades he has found it always

18

works, whereas more spectacular and complicated theories often don't.

In college his best friend, a popular Irish boy named Richard P. Lydon (later a New York Supreme Court Justice), was asked to join several Greek-letter fraternities but always declined while Baruch, although many times proposed, was always blackballed. "I don't think it was because I was disliked," he later said reflectively. "I think it was because I was a Jew." Yet if heredity had given him what was (in New York of the 1880's) a handicap, it had lavished on him good looks and a brain in which there was small room for morbid self-pity. And behind him there was a proudly solid family. "Remember," said his mother, as she started the boy out to Dick's sister's debutante party in his father's pinned-up dress suit, "that you are the handsomest boy in the world. The blood of princes is in your veins. Nobody is better than you, but you are no better than anyone else until you prove it."

So if a Jew could not then be a Greek-letter man, Bernard Baruch and Dick Lydon could run the senior class politics, with Bernie (working behind the scenes: it was to happen again) putting Dick in as president and himself becoming chairman of Class Day Exercises.

So then what? He had passed the examination for West Point but one bad ear (from a bat-blow in a half-forgotten baseball argument) kept him from possibly having become a general in World War I. Bob Fitzsimmons, who had watched his foot-work at Wood's gymnasium, was advising him to turn professional.

Yet a boy who at 18 could not only speak French and German but could read Latin, Hebrew and Homer in the original Greek, might aspire much higher. His father naturally wanted him to be a doctor but his mother, in doubt, marched him down to a popular phrenologist (a science as respected then as psychiatry is today) whose office was opposite what is now John Wanamaker's store. Dr. Fowler, who had a stately beard, professionally massaged the bumps on young Bernie's skull and then looked at his mother.

What did she propose to do with the young man? Mrs. Baruch mentioned medicine. The scientist shook his head. He could do not only this, but bigger things. They should consider finance or politics.

Only just how? Daniel Guggenheim, one of his father's patients, offered the boy a job buying ore in Mexico, but Mrs. Baruch again felt this was too far from home. So first he went to work (at $3 per week), using his long legs to run errands for a wholesale dealer in druggists' glassware, and thus caught his first glimpse of one of his heroes, old J. P. Morgan, Senior, whose huge, luminous red nose and fierce tawny eyes then dominated (and also stabilized) Wall Street.

Inevitably Baruch's next job was in this Street, working in an arbitration house where quickly he learned to convert any dollar amount into guilders, francs or sterling. But it seemed slow, and his 1890 summer job was working as a mucker, shovelling gold quartz into buckets at the bottom of a Cripple Creek mine shaft. Soon he was on the blasting crew. Then came the great chance to buy, with his savings, shares in a neighboring mine, where of course he immediately got a job. But with the poor ore he was now shovelling came his first investment lesson: never buy first and investigate later. He had been swindled, but in a nearby gambling house there might be a chance to recoup, by carefully placing small bets on the side of the house (it seemed to be making money). It was, but presently the proprietor, studying his methods, suggested that such patronage was unwanted.

"He seemed very much in earnest, so we left," Mr. Baruch remembers.

Back in New York and flat broke, he now went to work for the Wall Street firm of Arthur A. Hausman at $5 a week. First he only unlocked the office, kept the boss's inkwell filled and ran errands. But he was studying *Poor's Manual,* reading the *Financial Chronicle,* and soon could draw an industrial map of America, locating its railroads and industries, and recite their financial statements like the alphabet. Instead of looking up figures, they found at Hausman's, it was quicker (and just as accurate) to ask young Bernie. On the side he was studying law and bookkeeping in

21

night school. Useful things to know at Hausman's, where he was soon making the princely sum of $25 a week, which allowed for an occasional crack at the market. The trouble was, he would run his little stake up to two or three hundred dollars, and suddenly be wiped out.

But now James R. Keene, one of Hausman's customers and a big market operator of the day, noticed the boy, and first used him to place bets on the races over at Coney Island. Meanwhile the young man was courting Annie Griffen (and studying railway time tables and weather reports) as they sat together in Central Park. Because, as any beautiful girl should know, if a drought hit the corn crop, that would cut down Rock Island's earnings, whereas if a big rain should save the wheat crop, then this was the time to buy Union Pacific.

Anyone could see this, but Annie's parents were doubtful. It was a most substantial New York family (her father's money came from plate glass; her mother's from lard). The family was staunchly Episcopalian and the Griffens weren't sure about mixed marriages. Yet everybody liked Bernie.

With a bride in the offing, young Baruch asked the boss for a raise to $50 weekly—a dizzy sum for that day. Mr. Hausman parried, instead suggested a partnership, which on the basis of last year's figures would have meant $33 a week.

Young Baruch quickly accepted, and that year his partnership share was $6,000.

His family gasped in wonder and, in the flush of this success, the young man advised his father to invest $8,000 (a large part of the doctor's savings of 30 years) in stock of a streetcar company which the son knew was about to move. It did, all right, but downward. Every dollar of his father's savings went with it.

But this did not greatly matter for that year the son, shrewdly calculating that Congress would not cut the sugar tariff, bought heavily and made his first big killing of $60,000. That fall he married Annie Griffen in the Episcopal ring service, with brother Hartwig as best man, and paid $19,000 for a seat on the Exchange.

But this was only the start. The next year it happened that July 3rd fell on a Sunday and the young man was vacationing in Long Branch over the long Fourth of July weekend, when the stock markets would be closed. On this placid Sunday a call came from Hausman, who had a newspaper tip that our Commodore Schley had just destroyed Admiral Cervera's entire Spanish fleet in Santiago Bay. That meant the Spanish-American War was over and the market, when it finally opened, would go crazy. Perhaps young Baruch also remembered that, almost a century before, the great Rothschild fortune had been founded on an advance tip of Napoleon's defeat at Waterloo.

Carriages were too slow, so instantly he was on the phone hiring a locomotive which drew a single coach. On that flying trip to New York were Bernard Baruch, his youngest brother Saling and Hausman's brother Clarence. Because Saling was the slimest, they could boost him over the transom so that he could unlock the Hausman office.

Once inside young Bernie was on the telephone crank, passing on this inside tip to Hausman's oldest customers, cabling London (where they don't celebrate July 4th) in Hausman's name to buy, buy, buy American stocks the minute the British Exchange opened. Then they could all relax and wait for July 5th, when almost every stock on the American board surged upward, before deciding when to take their profit. It was a killing for every Hausman partner and customer. Could old Rothschild have thought faster?

So now the millions began to pile up. Thomas Fortune Ryan, a big Wall Street giant, was working to assemble a tobacco combine and put young Baruch in charge of raiding Continental, whose stock at the beginning stood at $45. For six weeks Baruch would first sell Continental short and then, when its stock tumbled, buy in at the bottom. When it recovered, he would again take his profit by selling on this crest. In six weeks Continental was down to $30.

"How much have you lost for me?" asked Ryan.

"I've made you a little."

Ryan shook his head. "Well, I want you to annoy them, but I don't want you to ruin them."

Presently young Baruch was on his way to St. Louis to buy Liggett & Myers for Ryan, and beat its owners down to a price of $12,000,000. His firm's commission for his work was $150,000.

Annie Griffen Baruch now had her own shiny black cabriolet with plate glass lamps and two liveried men on the box, when her husband heard a rumor that old Tom Ryan was investing heavily in American Spirits. Without thoroughly investigating either the rumor or the company, Baruch bet his shirt on American Spirits and lost every cent he had. They fired both footmen.

"I didn't tell you to buy," said Ryan gruffly. "Never pay attention to what I say to anybody else. A lot of people ask me questions who have no right to the answers."

Yet soon he was back and in the Street they were getting a respect for "Barnie" (after Barnie Barnato, a fabulous South African multi-millionaire of that day) and it was Old Jim Keene who, as the century turned (he was 60 and Baruch barely 30), told Mark Sullivan that Baruch was the greatest speculator of his generation. And it is Mark Sullivan himself who remembers Baruch of this period as "an eagle among eagles" in the Stock Exchange, making his money "with fierce swoops and darts, with quick twistings and turnings, in the strenuous and occasionally savage give-and-take."

In 1901 Baruch learned that Morgan and Harriman were fighting each other for control of Northern Pacific. What would happen? The stock would first soar as Morgan bid against Harriman and then, as the little fellows scrambled to get out of the way, it would drop. So Baruch first bought heavily and then—flip!—with exquisite timing he sold it and went short on the balance of the market, making money both on its rise and fall.

Again he heard (and again was right) that Jim Keene, William Rockefeller and a group of genial pirates who had working control of Amalgamated Copper, were going to take it for a buggy ride. Baruch was not of these insiders, but he hitch-hiked brilliantly —anticipating their tactics, buying as the stock soared to 130 and then selling short as it dropped to a bottom of 33.

But in the midst of this, one day after the market had closed, and Amalgamated's directors were scheduled to declare a dividend which might vitally affect his position, his desk telephone rang.

"Bernard," said his mother sternly, "have you forgotten what tomorrow is?"

Instantly he now remembered it was Yom Kippur, a sacred day on which no Jew may work or transact any business. The ultra-orthodox will not even snap an electric light switch (which is making a fire) between sunset and sunset. For Baruch it meant he could not even telephone the Street to protect himself on a day which might mean his ruin.

"I will expect you home," said his mother evenly.

"All right, mother."

All through Monday his friends on the Street tried to get him on the line, warning him to protect his position, but he would not answer their rings. Yet because Amalgamated continued downward, in the end he made $700,000 during a period which was later remembered by less agile brains as the Panic of 1901.

Cashing in his profits, he started on the first of what became his annual swings around the country, photographing and storing away, in that electronic brain, impressions of the surging industrial and agricultural growth of our young Republic; homesteaders breaking new sod, miners blasting into the Rockies, new railroad trestles spanning canyons; also getting the feel of its people.

In the prairie states men who had gambled on credit and lost were storming for "cheap money," more greenbacks, silver at 16 to 1, and denouncing "The Crime of '73."

What was the answer? Well, if something was wrong with this great and joyous (and constructive) poker game which was then our National Economy, maybe its rules should be changed, but not the value of the

27

chips, and only to benefit losers. Suppose a white chip were made equal to a blue one, how could it really help?

Thinking of this much later, he said, "I have studied paper dollars, silver dollars, commodity dollars, managed dollars. . . . They have not worked, and I do not think they will work. But gold has worked from Alexander s time down. When something holds good for 2,000 years, I do not believe it can be so because of prejudice, or a mistake in theory."

Yet what of his own life? By the time he was thirty-two he was proud of the fact that he "had $100,000 for every year of it." Surely money was an important measure of success.

How had his money come to him? First hear Baruch, who says impatiently, "I tell you, making money is purely and simply a faculty." Mark Sullivan, who was watching him, saw his ability as "something in the nature of artistic genius. Many a man who has made money doesn't conform to the characteristics of the business man. They make money as other men paint pictures or compose music. . . . I can't imagine anything that Baruch couldn't accomplish if he put his mind on it hard enough. . . . I can't imagine any game he couldn't win at, provided it interested him enough."

As for that of making money in the market, Baruch once reduced it to a few rules, some of which are:

1, 2, and 3: Don't speculate unless you make it your life work. Amateurs always go broke.

4: Never play tips from "insiders." They can't see the forest for the trees.

5: Keep a strong cash reserve and never trade on margins.

6: Never buy stock unless you know all about a company's officers, its bankers, its competitors and anything either in science or politics which may curtail its business.

7: Never hesitate to admit you are wrong, and don't talk about what you are doing, because pride may keep you from getting out and cutting your losses.

8: The time to buy is when the market is low, everyone is talking pessimistically, and no hope is in sight.

9: Sell when the market has had a long rise and is hesitating, with everybody in a frenzy of optimism. Don't be fooled by cats and dogs leaping up after the good stocks have hesitated.

10, 11, and 12: If a man buys a stock he thinks is going up, and then the ticker starts saying, "You're wrong—you're wrong—you're wrong!", you may judge his ability as a speculator by the length of time it takes the ticker to convince him.

Another Baruch practice which might be a rule is, when a market operation is finished, to liquidate completely, salt the profits down in cash or bonds ("where it won't forget who owns it") and then often to take a train out of town, to "soar off like an eagle, circle high above men to look things over."

In this period he was sorely irritated (perhaps also hurt) because his sincere admiration for J. P. Morgan the Elder had to be conducted from a respectful distance, since this august financial statesman regarded him disdainfully as a "successful gambler."

In point of fact as his (and Woodrow Wilson's) old friend George Creel has pointed out, "No man was ever less a gambler" and another shrewd witness is Herbert Bayard Swope, who says that, in important matters, "Bernie is like an elephant at a bridge. He tests every board with the utmost care, and after he is fully satisfied that it will bear his weight, sits down on the bank and waits for somebody else to go across first."

He delights to bet on horse races, elections and straight flushes only after he has eliminated all possible elements of chance, and it might be said that no one will gamble with more spectacular recklessness on a proposition which (following careful investigation) he finally knows is a sure thing.

Yet even in the new office at 111 Broadway he was restless. Money was an important measure of success, but what did you do with it? Well, you could, for instance, start reassembling Hobcaw Barony down in South Carolina near Georgetown, which was first a royal grant of 10,000 acres to Lord Carteret, and was then owned by generations of Hugers and Alstons until it slipped from their hands in the Civil War. It was wasteland now, with mallard and teal duck blackening the marshes in season, deer and wild turkey in the forests, and bob-white quail on the high pastures. Bit by bit he began buying it up. Was he fleeing to this little private monarchy to escape New York taxes?

"Not on your life!" he exploded to George Creel. "I still owe and will always owe for the free education given me in New York's public schools."

Yet still he was restless, as shrewd friends could see. "You know, B.M.," said Garet Garrett (then a financial reporter, later a *Saturday Evening Post* editor), "you're not really a Wall Street man at heart. You should go into public life: some day you will."

But in 1903 this seemed a crazy guess, for more joyous battles were to be won in the Street and in industry. He had been nosing into statistics on copper, and one day told the Guggenheims, "You fellows don't know what you've got." Because, compared to their future, copper stocks were underpriced. So next year Old Dan gave him the job of buying Takoma Smelter (the Rockefellers were also bidding) which he finally delivered in a neat package. Sam Untermyer, the Guggenheim's lawyer, then brought up the matter of the fee.

"One million dollars," said B.M., which Untermyer

felt might be a matter for discussion. But Old Dan Guggenheim did not agree.

"If Bernie says he ought to get a million, that's what he will get."

Out of it of course came some expenses, and B.M. sent checks for $300,000 each to Henry Davis and William Rust, two men who had helped him handle the Westerners. Both were amazed, for they felt they had done little, but he refused to let them send back the money.

If the following year he lost in coffee (he discovered his would not grade) he made it up with a gold mine, which accounts for the fact that the Panic of 1907 found him with more than two million cash squirrelled away in his safety deposit boxes.

Despair stalked the land, and Morgan the Elder was rising to the Responsibilities of Financial Statesmanship by raising a fund to plug the runs on "sound" banks, unsound ones being no concern of the Morgans. Years later Old J.P. was to learn that an anonymous million of it had come from this "successful gambler." Other friends were having trouble getting cash to meet the smelter payroll of what is now the Kennicott Copper Co., so B.M. opened another little hoard of half a million in folding money, which quickly went west by express. Then he turned around and bought all he could in the market at $15 and $16 a share.

Just before the panic, probing into rubber, Dan

Guggenheim had become convinced that the British and Dutch out in the Far East were pegging the price too high, so he invited Baruch, Nelson Aldrich and Tom Ryan to put up something short of a million each to form Continental Rubber which, they hoped, might do with rubber what already had been done by Rockefeller with oil. One source was guayule, but where did this little bush thrive best? Baruch went to Mexico to talk it over with President Diaz, sent expeditions to Borneo, up the Amazon and over the Andes, and also probed into Belgian Congo, then the private fief of Leopold I, where Baruch found that the King maintained labor conditions which were almost as spectacularly scandalous as His Majesty's private life. And although this monarch did not give a damn about public opinion, he was told that Belgian Congo must have a sociological house-cleaning before prudent American capital would invest.

Then in 1909 came an even bigger chance, for he was approached by the august House of Morgan, which suggested he inspect a sulphur dome in Brazoria County, Texas. When he returned, he was ushered directly into The Presence, and reported that the property stood a 50-50 chance of paying off, could be had for half a million, of which Baruch himself would be willing "to gamble half."

It was not a happy phrase. Of course Old J.P.'s tiger-eyes glared out at the young upstart from under their

33

shaggy grey brows and over the bridge of that iridescent nose.

"I never gamble," he growled. That ended the interview.

But it did not end the deeply humiliated young man's interest in sulphur. Taking the chance the House of Morgan turned down (although they came in later), Baruch founded Texas Gulf Sulphur at an original cost of $10 for each share which sold, on the crest of the 1929 boom, at a price equivalent to $340 a share.

It was nice to be right, to be able to replace Annie Griffen Baruch's black cabriolet first with a French Panhard (suitably equipped with a Parisian chauffeur) and then with a $22,000 yellow Mercedes parked outside their brownstone mansion on 52d Street near the University Club.

Except that, as he told an old friend of the period, "Every afternoon at 6 o'clock my father-in-law drives up to that Club, gets out and goes in. But I can't be a member." Now was this largely because, as he added, "I'm a Jew," or was it somewhat because there were others besides the Elder Morgan who shared that heavily Anglican view of Bernard Baruch as only "a successful gambler"?

It was pleasant, at 40 to have outsiders estimate one's fortune as surely not less than ten million, and possibly fifteen. Yet money was only one measure of success, for his venerated father had relatively little of it to show for a lifetime of service to human suffering.

What lay beyond? It was like Guggenheim's story of the crazy little man who somehow got into old Meyer's office, trying to sell him some new smelting process. In excited German the little man clamored that, with this process, Mr. Guggenheim could control all the copper in the world. Old Meyer was unmoved. And control of copper would bring control of all other metals. Still Old Dan was unexcited. But couldn't he see, screamed the little man, that controlling all metals, he would become a Colossus—the richest, the most powerful man in the whole world!

Old Meyer Guggenheim leaned over his desk with a wry smile and pulled his side-whiskers.

"Und dann?" he had asked.

So what else could life hold for one who, in his early forties, was already a multi-millionaire? As it turned out, an idealistic professor in nearby Princeton had part of the answer to this mystery.

PART TWO

Baruch and
Woodrow Wilson
(1912-1929)

IT WAS REALLY HIS FATHER, DR. SIMON Baruch, who made the decision for him. The old man knew that the son had always avoided public honors, but to be asked to accept a trusteeship of C.C.N.Y. was something more. It was a duty which could not be evaded, and in finally accepting, Bernard Baruch stumbled into a chain of circumstances which changed his life.

How else could he have met William F. McCombs, who was not only a fellow-trustee, not only the Democratic Party's future National Chairman, but a devoted admirer of Woodrow Wilson who, first with his fight against snobbery in Princeton's eating clubs and then with his book, *The New Freedom,* was attracting national praise.

There was the further fact that the Republican Party was hopelessly split over Theodore Roosevelt so that in the election of 1912 the Democrats (out of office now since Cleveland) would have a better than even chance. In the spring Billie McCombs asked him to come up to the Plaza to meet Governor Wilson and Colonel House (a sulphur dome, a race horse, a gold mine or a man: he wants to see for himself) and he announced next day that he had "met one of the few Great Men of the world," a judgment which never changed. On Wilson's part, a friendship began here which outlasted the trust he gave to William Jennings Bryan, to his son-in-law, McAdoo, to Colonel E. M. House, to Robert Lansing and even to his devoted secretary, Joe Tumulty.

Why? First Wilson appreciated the depth and brilliance of a mind which had mastered Morgan's Wall Street and Homer's Greek. Secondly, here was a capitalist who owned shares in companies which many people thought would be ruined by Wilson's program, and yet who told Wilson that he was right; who in return asked nothing but gave much, and always anonymously (to Wilson's second campaign a total of $50,000) and to Wilson personally he gave the obedience of a son.

Most important of all he gave sound advice. When Wilson's bill establishing our Federal Reserve System hit a rebellious Congress, it was Baruch, sitting in the Round Room, who coaxed the square-jawed Presbyterian into accepting some little amendments, without which the bill would have been lost.

And if Bernard Baruch enjoyed Washington, a growing circle of Wilsonian Democrats, both in the Cabinet and in Congress, began to enjoy the moss-hung, natural magnificence of Hobcaw, its miles of white beaches, its teeming groves of game, and to marvel at the four tiny Negro villages in which Mr. Baruch operates as a one-man Welfare State, supplying his tenants with milk, with free doctors, and even on occasion (when they felt like it) with work, which is usually the task of repairing their own cabins.

There was bounty for all, even for visiting Admiral Grayson who, no matter how many of B.M.'s shot-gun shells he pumped through B.M.'s guns, seemed never to be able to hit even one of B.M.'s wild turkeys. So came a day when the guide pointed out to him— up through the bearded branches—the outline of a huge gobbler. The Admiral cleared for action, blew to battle-stations, elevated his turrets, let fly with a broadside, there was a crackling of twigs, a thump on the moss, where at last lay a magnificent fowl, the card around its neck reading, "with the Compliments of Bernard M. Baruch."

Meanwhile Europe had blundered into World War I, which quickly divided America, first with Southern Senators storming at the British for interfering with their cotton market. But then, as bubbles from the *Lusitania* arose, Senator Henry Cabot Lodge, shaking his white spike beard in rage, replied that "A dead baby floating on the water is a more poignant sight to me than an unsold bale of cotton."

Quietly as always, Baruch had offered to contribute

41

3 million to McAdoo's fund to finance surplus cotton. Meanwhile he had taken a plunge on his own into gold mines, organizing (in 1915 with Eugene Meyer, Jr.,) Alaska Juneau, with the proud announcement that the two would take, at $10 a share, "all stock not taken by public subscription." And why into gold? Because, possibly dating from the days when he saw that drawerful of Confederate money in old Saling Wolfe's house at Winnsboro, he has felt this yellow metal to be (along with art works and good farm land) one of the few permanent investments in this uncertain world.

One shrewd Rothschild, setting up a permanent trust fund, had cautiously spread his investment among gilt-edged British, French, Austrian and German bonds, only to see it shrink to one-fifth its value. And if gold yields no interest, Baruch points out that in the hoardings of the Maharajahs today are gold staters brought to India by Alexander of Macedon in the Fourth Century before Christ. These princes may have missed two millenniums of interest. Yet, had they speculated, how many times in those 2,000 years would they have gone broke?

But for fifteen years Bernard Baruch seemed wrong, for Alaska Juneau's ore was poor ("I put up 3 million to get that company out of a hole") and when by 1920 the stock had dropped to 75 cents a share, most of his friends had let go. Baruch held on.

Meanwhile he was running into political troubles. Rumors from the trench-bound European front of victories, defeats and peace-feelers were fluttering the American market, in which he was intermittently operating and with some success. In late 1916 a Peace note sent by Wilson caused a sharp price break. Embittered bulls started the rumor that Baruch had been cleaning up (this was true) because, as Wilson's friend, he had had advance news (he had none) of the President's plans. Hitherto Baruch's name had appeared only briefly on financial pages—"B. M. Baruch led the shorts today." Now headlines splashed out the charge that this sinister, market-rigging gambler had capitalized on his friendship with the White House idealist to clean up in the Street. Republicans sharpened their knives.

But at the investigating committee hearing, he laid it on the line. When asked his occupation, he said firmly:

"I am a speculator."

Arthur Krock remembers "a remarkably handsome man, six feet two, spare in figure, gentle in speech, white of hair, grey of eye, who not only admitted but *asserted* that he was a market operator, and tried to make all the money he could out of it." One who didn't need to buy or betray government secrets, since he could take care of himself.

But just how?

Well, there was December 18, 1916, when, in an uneasy market, men were hanging over the ticker to read a speech British Premier Lloyd George was making to Parliament. The Allies, the little Welchman was saying, would fight on to victory, "but—" and at that instant, without waiting for the sentence to end, Baruch had swiftly given the order to sell 25,000 shares of U. S. Steel. For that word "but" could only mean Lloyd George was about to give some hint of peace which would for the moment chill America's roaring munitions prosperity. Baruch's split-second speed had made him almost half a million dollars that afternoon. "I wish," said a wistful Congressman, "you could teach me how to do it."

The complete vindication led to his appointment in July, 1917, to a high position in the Council of National Defense. Why at last did he accept a public office? Professor Alvin Johnson (then an economist for the Council) feels that "what ground on Bernie was the fact that his career appeared to be essentially acquisitive . . . He had nothing to impress on the public his essentially creative character." The appointment was not instantly popular. The New York *Annalist* observed that "his name is not in Who's Who . . . he does not hold a line in the Directory of Directors . . . a big speculator in stocks; a gambler . . ." and such an appointment "would have been impossible in any other day" perhaps because, as Clinton Gilbert (*Mirrors of Washington*) pointed out, he came from "that part of Wall Street which is beyond the pale; he did not belong to the right moneyed set."

The nation's most widely quoted political writer, Mark Sullivan, felt that "for the President to give Baruch the office . . . involved a good deal of courage" because "among that section of the voters who regard money-making careers with distrust, Baruch's method is . . . most looked down upon. He organized no corporations, created no factories, built no railroads."

Faced with the task of spending an estimated 10 billion dollars in American and Allied money on food and munitions, Baruch's first step was to sell every share of stock in any company he owned which might be affected by government action. The rest he put into a trust fund whose proceeds went to war charities. "I've known Bernie to give a million dollars to the Red Cross," says Herbert Hoover, "without any public announcement then or later."

And as for the Council, if it was at the outset hamstrung by disputes between Army and Navy and was therefore, as Alvin Johnson saw it, "little more than a knitting society with no power," it brought Baruch into daily contact with President Wilson, who first named him "Dr. Facts" and later observed, "Two

45

kinds of people came to Washington: one that swelled and one that grew. Baruch grew."

As for the President, even in Princeton they had observed that "it makes Wilson sick at his stomach to be contradicted," and now in Washington Mark Sullivan observed that most men who came in close contact with Wilson, "make him ill at ease. He prefers to talk only to those who see the idealist in himself. . . . He doesn't like to talk to people who argue with him," so that, within the White House it was Mr. Baruch's natural humility, "the kind of humility that would have saved Wilson," as Clinton Gilbert remembers, "that served Mr. Baruch there."

But outside the White House Mark Sullivan quickly predicted that "Baruch promises to be the whole works here in Washington." He had "pulled the reins out of everybody else's hands, and is flying down the road with his tail over the dashboard. When there isn't any money available, he uses his own. When his secretary complained they needed more space, Baruch said, 'Buy the building.' . . . With all his assumption of authority, he doesn't get anyone mad at him. He is always ready to compromise or change the program . . . to get something . . . his good nature and boyishness and enthusiasm are helpful to him."

With these assets he presently was able to show the President that the chaos could only be ended with a grant of real power, so in the spring of 1918 the knitting society became the War Industries Board with Bernard Baruch its chairman.

For his associates Baruch had men like Alexander Legge, Rear Admiral Fletcher, Major General Goethals (he had built the Panama Canal; later Hugh Johnson took his place), George N. Peek for the farmers, J. Leonard Replogle (steel), Albert C. Ritchie and Herbert Bayard Swope. Observers of that day doubt that there was ever a time when Baruch himself added up a column of figures; his genius lay in getting Replogle to take over steel, Summers to ride herd on chemicals, Legge to manage production, keeping their loyalty, arbitrating their differences, soaking up their statistics, hearing their arguments and then making final decisions.

Public opinion on Bernard Baruch had now moved a pace. "The very facts urged against his original appointment," said Commerce and Finance, "are reasons why he is one of the best men that could have been selected" for this promotion. "Yes, Baruch is a Jew and he is proud of it." But feeling on this score was bound to yield because of the "public spirit and the patriotism he displayed" and Wall Street had even "accused him of being a Socialist in his devotion to the interests of the people as represented by the government."

John Hancock, who in those days worked with Baruch for the Navy (in World War II he was to serve

47

him in connection with the Rubber Survey and the later Atomic Energy Board), recalls that Baruch's great strength lay in the fact that, as a speculator, he had come to know "the leader of every important industry and the reputation of every man for integrity. He also knew the peacetime production figures of every industry within 10 per cent—had them in his head, so if we came in with a big war order, Baruch knew exactly what this would do to civilian supply." .

Alvin Johnson, then a young WIB statistician, also testifies that because Baruch had been a speculator, he knew "the working of industry, . . . the stuffed shirts that man the window display . . . the key men who make industries work. He built on the key men."

As for his new powers, President Wilson had written him that "the ultimate decision of all questions . . . should rest always with the chairman." But John Hancock remembers that Baruch gave his associates (after carefully picking them) "absolute power. If the politicians attacked us, he felt they were attacking him, and went to bat. If he thought his associates were too buoyant or too depressed, he leveled them off. You could always get an attentive hearing if he thought you knew what you were talking about."

A supporting later witness on the elusive methods of Baruch's brilliant mind is Fred Eberstadt, a World War II associate, who points out that "Bernie doesn't study elaborate statistical reports. He gets the results by word of mouth, or succinct memorandum. His ability to inspire advice and then weigh it are his attributes of greatness. He is never overwhelmed or confused by a mass of facts. You would never say of him, 'He's a busy man'—always seems to have time to talk to everybody. There is also his great sensitivity to people—his extraordinary courtesy and thoughtfulness. His secretary does not have to remind him that this is your birthday—the warmest personality I ever knew—and he's never dogmatic until, having soaked up all the digested facts, he makes up his mind."

There is also his subconscious mind, his brilliant and seemingly effortless hunches—the fact that Muscle Shoals, which might answer America's nitrate problem, came to him one morning in a dream. It has fascinated all who have been close to him. The dazzled Hugh Johnson complained that "Bernie's judgments come forth spontaneously like lightning, with no supporting brief of argument." But Mr. Baruch, who follows his own subconscious with that blind faith which the ancient Romans placed in auguries and sheep's entrails, insists that "to have a hunch, you must first have all the facts at your command, and your intelligence must be working at full speed. Then suddenly and without conscious effort you think of a solution which is really based on facts, but isn't achieved by deliberate cerebrations. With it comes an unexampled feeling of well-being."

49

This brain, directing the above-listed team, housed in a temporary clapboard two-by-four and tar-paper building in Washington, tackled the job of gearing America's industrial production for World War I.

An early hurdle was to get an agreement with Steel —whose leaders inevitably wanted more per ton. Price-fixing agreements were supposed to be voluntary, but Wilson had whispered to Baruch, "Let the manufacturer see the club behind your door . . ." So presently Steel (Judge Elbert Gary, Charlie Schwab, Eugene Grace and about 40 others) gathered in that temporary building "whose paper walls," John Hancock remembers, "were so thin you could hear the man in the next room change his mind." There was a lot of discussion, but when Baruch came on the scene, sharp-eyed, diamond-encrusted Broadway sparrow, Billy Rose, then in his teens and Baruch's stenographer, still remembers that "they all respected and trusted him—he was Papa!"

Just what Baruch said was not known for years, but when Steel, after listening, came out of its huddle, John Hancock remembers that little, white-haired Judge Gary began speaking "in a low-pitched monotone with his words spaced about a foot apart, saying that, while not one of the 40 approved the government's views, still they were accepting them."

Why? Years later it leaked out. Mr. Baruch, with exquisite tact, had hinted that it would cause the government much trouble and himself deep personal sorrow if he were forced to nationalize the industry. So Steel decided to spare him this pain.

There was also our Allies, and Baruch's opposite number in London was the youngest member of Lloyd George's Coalition government, Winston Churchill, Minister of Munitions. He had not yet met Baruch, but testifies that "almost daily telegrams put us on excellent terms. I could feel at the other end of the cable a strong, clear mind, taking quick decisions and standing by them."

Inevitably there were disagreements, Baruch feeling that the British Dominion of India was asking us an outrageous price for jute. In Washington the British shrugged. How could they control India?

"Once upon a time," Baruch told them, "a Negro and a bear met on a narrow path. 'Oh, Lord!' said the Negro, 'help me. But if you don't help me, don't help the bear, and you'll see a hell of a fight!' " What could the big Yankee mean?

They found out when it was presently rumored America might ban exports of silver, which was bolstering India's currency. If this collapsed, we could buy jute cheaply in terms of her depreciated rupees. Quickly the British found they could bring India to reason.

Likewise the neutral Chileans thought they had us over the barrel for nitrates, and the price was soaring.

51

So at this point came Baruch's dream. Why not, with cheap electricity which could be had from Muscle Shoals, suck nitrate from the air, and make America forever self-sufficient? For Chile, Baruch's dream was a sheet-ripping nightmare, and quickly the price dropped.

From neutral Spain, then languishing under the heel of Alphonso XIII, and in return for badly needed ammonium phosphate fertilizer, he extorted the number of artillery mules necessary, in that unmechanized era, to make the world safe for Democracy. Mr. Baruch in essence invented economic warfare.

He was about to move to rip the steel from women's corsets, to abolish pleasure cars, pocket flaps, to reduce shoe types to 3; to put civilians into cheap but serviceable uniforms under rationing and pegged prices so that all could buy, when unexpectedly World War I ended. But in ten months our shipbuilding capacity had increased ten-fold, we had stepped up our overseas shipments of troops from 70,000 to 300,000 a month, we were prepared, in the next 12 months, to make 100,000 airplanes. We had sent France steel for 160 million .75 shells and food to feed 12,000,000 Frenchmen for 18 months. No small factor in Germany's surrender was America's "brilliant if pitiless war industry" as Field Marshal von Hindenburg later wrote, which "had not failed it."

When on October 7, 1918, Wilson learned from the

Swiss that the Germans were ready to make peace on the basis of his Fourteen Points, he gave word to Baruch quietly to begin folding up our economic war.

In conclusion Baruch did two things. The WIB had taken from modest homes throughout the land about 5,000 girl clerks and stenographers, dazzled with Washington's wartime gaiety and now jobless in the Big City. Baruch, concerned (as a Southern gentleman would be) with their morals, privately engaged to pay (for those who could not afford it) their rail fares home. The $4,500 came from his own pocket. Secondly, he sent President Wilson a long outline for a skeletal peacetime organization, linking government and industry in case of future war: Congress, which thought the peace would last for millenniums, was uninterested. Had Baruch's plan been adopted, it would have saved billions in World War II. For not until 1943 did we finally give Donald Nelson (Baruch's later counterpart) the necessary authority which Baruch was wielding in the spring of 1918.

When Wilson presently sailed for Paris, he wanted Baruch at his side, for his peace would have economic problems no less pressing than those of war.

The plate glass windows of the stately Hotel Crillon, which housed the American delegation, not only gave on Louis XIV's majestic Place de la Concorde, with the Chambre des Deputees distantly across the Seine, but surveyed the blazing uniforms of the victors and the babel of their conflicting aims.

In all of allied Europe, the politicians had promised their peoples that defeated Germany would pay not only for War Damage, but also every sou, farthing, kopek and centissimo of Allied War Costs, including even war pensions into the distant future.

Baruch was not blind to the claims of justice or vengeance, but was more interested in facts. These were that a completely crushed Germany could not pay reparations: little milk can be stripped from the udder of a dead cow. Also, Germany could pay only by exporting; had the victorious statesmen stopped to think that the necessary tidal wave of cheap German goods might bankrupt their domestic industries?

They had not, nor indeed could they. For each had been elected on a promise that Germany would pay all; each now feared even to present his nation's bill lest a rival politician say it was too low.

Towering, fierce-eyed old French Premier Georges Clemenceau, that veteran of the 1870 Commune whose shiny bald pate now moved unsteadily under the crystal chandeliers of the Salle des Mirrors, had at first liked Baruch, a man of his own stature both in height and brain, and had dubbed him "le Prince d'Israel." Yet as Baruch, in the Supreme Economic Council, continued to talk not vengeance but deflating arithmetic on what might be reasonably expected of the Germans, all France screamed that he was pro-Boche. It was even whispered that he and McAdoo were questioning Allied good faith in the matter of their war debts to America. So, in the purple velvet-carpeted ante-rooms, swallow-tailed backs were studiously turned on Dr. Facts until one climactically bitter day, as a conference was breaking up, and Baruch was standing forlorn on the Quai d'Orsay steps, a frail white hand engaged his arm.

"Ride home with me," said the President of the United States.

"He is the most Christ-like man," said Baruch later (it is his highest measure of praise), "that I ever knew."

Back in America the Frail Man, preaching his League of Nations, made his final tour, pleading to the listless audiences, bored now with war and with European entanglements, which gathered around the brass rail of his observation car as he bitterly charged that those who were opposing his League were "breaking the heart of the world." Then when the Frail Man himself collapsed at Trinidad, Colorado, and was silently rushed home to Washington, Baruch undertook a survey of the nation, to discover that opposition to Wilson and his League was serious, but not quite hopeless.

The disaffected groups included pacifists and isolationists who were clustered about William Jennings Bryan, Germans who thought Wilson had betrayed the

Vaterland by abandoning his 14 points, Italians who thought Jugoslavia had no rights in Fiume, and the normally Democratic Irish who resented the fact that in the League's Assembly Britain and her dominions would have six votes and America only one.

Yet Baruch was sure these all could be placated if Wilson would only give a little face-saving ground. After all, a compromise had saved his Federal Reserve bill. Returning to Washington Baruch was the first person outside the immediate family to stand by the Frail Man's bed in the White House, there to repeat the assurance of several Senators that the necessary two-thirds vote for his League of Nations could be had if Wilson would only accept Taft's reservation to the League's tenth article.

The Frail Man struggled up from his pillows. The old flexibility which had let him compromise on the Federal Reserve Act had vanished with his health.

Article 10, he snapped, was the heart of the League. If he accepted this nullifying reservation, he would be false to every young man who lay dead in Flanders. Or so it then seemed to that sick mind, just groping its way back from the shadows of a recent brain hemorrhage. What more could Baruch or any other man have said and keep his friendship? And also, "He was right," says Baruch, "as we now see."

So months passed and the League was defeated in the Senate, the Frail Man in the sick room never quite realizing that his own petty obstinacy had killed his dream. At the height of his illness the Senate even talked of impeachment, and Mark Sullivan, that era's crack reporter, put the question as to who was actually acting as President at this moment, telling the Frail Man which bills should and should not be signed. Sullivan found the answer was that "a group—Secretary Tumulty, Rear Admiral Grayson and Bernard Baruch" formed a Regency Council which was in effect governing America in Woodrow Wilson's name.

Yet presently all of it was swept away in the 1920 landslide for Harding and "normalcy," the Frail Man leaving the White House to linger a few fitful years in his S Street home, and Baruch returning to New York.

What now remained? His taste of public life under Wilson had given him, as Clinton Gilbert shrewdly remarked, "a profound distaste for mere money-making." Yet during the ensuing twelve Republican years under Harding, Coolidge, and Hoover, his opportunities for public service were understandably limited. There was his fortune which, at the war's end, would list at $8\frac{1}{2}$ millions in Liberty Bonds, better than a million in Texas Gulf and his other permanent investments, plus his customary safety deposit squirrel-pile of cash, making a total of 10 millions.

Money-making has been sporadically for him a joyous game like poker, yet he felt that, because as wartime chairman of WIB he had learned so many industrial secrets, it would not now be ethical to amuse himself in the stock market.

So far as the public was concerned, America, having pulled out of Europe, was entering an eon of peace. Baruch did not believe it. So when the 1920 Congress set up a skeleton industrial mobilization plan in case of another war, plus an Industrial War College, Baruch plunged avidly in. He and his old WIB subordinates, John Hancock and Hugh S. Johnson, gave frequent lectures there to army and navy officers. There was a promising youngster called Dwight Eisenhower ("His papers were always at the top when I was lecturing at the college," Baruch remembers), and every time the army produced a new quartermaster general, it was up to this experienced civilian team tactfully to whip him into shape.

Also Baruch was a lone voice for preparedness, frequently appearing before Congressional Committees lecturing them as to how, if (Baruch said when) War came again, to avoid 1917's chaos. As for peace, he financed at Williamstown, Mass., a School of International Relations where the world's leading statesmen and economists came to lecture and diagnose the world's ills.

Then annually (until after World War II) the Würzburger flowed at lavish luncheons of the old WIB crowd gathered to salute "The Chief," with the irrepressible Herb Swope as toastmaster interrupting speeches unless slapped down by Baruch: "Don't Swope unless you're Swopen to!"

Post-war agriculture was staggering under the problem of surpluses and low prices and the Kansas Board of Agriculture in 1920 appealed to Baruch for advice. Following a survey, he struck at the problem's heart in a report recommending scientific crop-marketing—"the bulk of [the farmer's] output comes on the market . . . at a time when . . . both freight cars and money are scarce." The answer? More elevator space, built either privately or through cooperatives which might also arrange with banks for cheaper crop-financing, getting low bulk prices for both just as big business does.

Finding further that farmers were frequently getting short weight and under-grading, he recommended that this be done by "impartial and disinterested public inspectors." He also urged that farmers should have "freedom to integrate the business of agriculture . . . consolidate selling agencies . . . to put the farmer on an equal footing with the large buyers of his product."

Lastly "the Department of Agriculture should collect . . . and distribute to the farmers full information from all the markets of the world," so that the man who raised the crop should be as well-informed as the market traders.

And his fee? "Not a penny now or ever," as the farm leaders told it later. "Mr. Baruch said our confidence was his retainer." Later he shocked Wall Street by backing his farmer-friends in support of their McNary-Haugen Bill, a plan for price-pegging plus dumping abroad (the cost of which the farmers would bear) which he held to be "absolutely sound" in that it would "hold down over-planting of wheat." It infuriated Harding and Coolidge but the farmers replied, "Bernie Baruch is for it, I guess he knows something about business and finance, doesn't he?"

Before the 1924 Democratic Convention Baruch backed Wilson's son-in-law, William J. McAdoo. The Harding oil scandals were rocking the nation: surely the Democrats could win. But the convention ended in an exhausting deadlock between Al Smith and McAdoo followed by a party split (wet-dry, Klan and anti-Klan) and Baruch then vowed never again to support a candidate before the Convention.

Republican Washington was not quite a total blackout for Baruch. He had written a book on war debts and reparations "as dull"—his friend, Arthur Krock, pointed out—"as [British economist] Keynes is brilliant, and as accurate as Keynes is inaccurate," he tried to interest the White House in the realities of world economics. Harding had been expansively pleasant (but had understood nothing), Coolidge had only listened. Slowly Baruch began to see that no administration could afford to cancel war debts with the public soured on Europe: "They hired the money, didn't they?" Coolidge had asked: this was the popular note. When

Baruch suggested they might write off the debt for arms and count only money lent after the war, Coolidge thanked him: that was all.

But presently came a winter when Baruch, Swope and Krock were on their way to a Florida vacation and when at Washington a uniformed official boarded their car.

"Mr. Baruch, the President [Coolidge] wishes to have lunch with you."

From the White House under any President this was an order, so Baruch left the train. The lamb chops were skimpy, the peas overcooked, the conversation spotty. Then they went into the President's office.

"You have sat in that chair before, Mr. Baruch."

"Yes, that was my chair when Mr. Wilson was President."

"Mr. Baruch, you are a patriot."

"Yes, I claim that I am."

"If the President of the United States asks your help in a matter of foreign affairs, you give it."

"Yes, Mr. President, if I can."

"I need your help in the settlement of the Italian debt situation. I need Democratic support in the Senate. Will you help me put it through?"

"Yes, Mr. President, since that is the situation."

It was agreed that temporarily he could go to Florida. On his first night there, during a poker game with Swope and Krock, he told them with quiet pride of the assignment. Toward midnight when, by a coincidence, he was $12,000 in the hole (he hates to lose) a bellboy entered.

"Mr. Baruch, the President of the United States wants you on the phone."

The famous Baruch intuition now worked at top speed. Since hearing the Washington news, both Krock and Swope had made thin excuses to leave the room. Either could have tipped the bellboy to break up this game while Baruch was behind.

So he fixed the bellboy with a piercing eye. "You tell the President of the United States from me," he said, "to go to hell." And he returned to his cards. Naturally Krock and Swope both protested that he should break off. But now he was doing better, an hour later was only $9,000 behind when the boy entered again.

"Mr. Baruch, Secretary Mellon wishes to speak to you."

"You tell Secretary Mellon to go to hell." The first time it might have been funny. But why should Swope and Krock keep up their childish game? Next morning as he came down to breakfast, the hotel clerk said: "Mr. Baruch, Secretary Mellon wishes you to call him."

He took the next train for Washington, first saw the Republicans, and then laid down the law to his old Hobcaw duck-hunting friends in the Senate.

"What, 27 Democrats!" they protested. The bill would be most unpopular. "There aren't 27 Democrats who could afford to vote for it!"

But in the end 27 were persuaded, and when the bill passed, not a newspaper criticized it.

As the peaceful twenties rolled on, in an occasional speech or magazine article he would hammer home his warning that in case of war, the President should have power to freeze all prices and wages as of some date at its beginning, making it illegal to "buy, sell, hire, serve or rent at any other." After all, the price of any one thing depends on the price of everything. Piecemeal price-fixing would be impossible, only wholesale pegging of the entire structure could stave off inflation. So he pleaded, but in the placid twenties, who cared?

Occasionally he would warn of the booming market. "The speculator . . . is a dealer in realities." There were "many great forces working day and night to undermine our best judgments, to put to test our most careful deliberations . . . Debt settlements, crops, foreign exchange, British labor troubles . . . everything may be progressing smoothly when a sudden upheaval in Russia, in France . . . breaks the continuity of progress."

But toward the end of 1927 he dealt himself a hand in this big game. There was no shortage of chips, for that investment in Texas Gulf Sulphur (on which old J. P. Morgan had refused to gamble) had trebled his fortune. His first step was to hire, as his bird-dog and research assistant, General Hugh S. Johnson whom he had sized up in WIB days.

His second was to give Johnson a lecture in their 57th Street office which made Johnson furious.

"Stay away from that ticker," commanded Baruch. "You cannot do your best job if you are worrying about the movements of stock prices." And Johnson's job? To look into companies for things which in the future would make them move, on the basis of which, Baruch would either invest or stay out.

Johnson remembered that eventually he looked into such divergent fields as rayon production, Bird's Eye and other artificial refrigeration processes, air conditioning, the movie industry, several hydro-electric projects and department stores, as well as the soft-drink industry. But during his first week, "Bernie, in one of his seemingly clairvoyant flashes, gave a prophecy of what was to come . . . the inflationary boom, the unbearable burden of foreign debt, the foolishness of foreign loans, their eventual repudiation and the coming of the deluge. He did not attempt to time it. He said that could not be done." But, "Watch automobile sales and the construction figures," Baruch had said. "This whole false fabric is built on the unprecedented conjunction of these two big credit-inflated booms—when they slide, the whole structure will collapse."

So Johnson watched them "as a cat watches a rat-hole."

PART THREE

Baruch and F.D.R.

(1929-1945)

As THE 1929 BOOM APPROACHED, BARUCH bought and sold, always, as Hugh Johnson noticed, "with his lines of retreat left open, and his weather eye on the gathering clouds," because Johnson's 1928 studies were showing that in spite of the booming stock market and inflated profits of a few companies, "the bulk of manufacture was operating in the red, with no less than 3 million employables out of work."

Yet no one could say when the bomb would burst, and in the brief interim Professor Alvin Johnson, a friend from WIB days, has a vivid memory of the day the Chief was sailing for France, and he had called to wish him Godspeed. As can happen with those close to Baruch, he suddenly found himself whirled off as a voyage companion, but just before the sailing the phone rang in Baruch's room.

"What's that!" roared Baruch. "You say I'm holding you up? Just for that, the price will be two million more." He cracked down the receiver.

Three days out as they were pacing the liner's promenade deck, Baruch was saying, "Now I'll tell you just where Ricardo fell down—" when:

"Radiogram for Mr. Baruch! Radiogram for Mr. Baruch!"

When the envelope was slit, Johnson could not help seeing it was an acceptance of this extra two million price, added in anger.

"Now this," continued Mr. Baruch, "is just where Ricardo fell down. Ricardo didn't take into consideration—"

Yet into the record must now go one curious item. "Watch automobile sales and construction figures," the Chief had warned in late 1927. Faithful Hugh Johnson was presumably still at his rat hole. Then in the spring of 1929 as we blindly drifted toward the chasm's brink, Mr. Baruch bloomed into print with something which was half analysis and half prophecy, in that solid business man's bible, *The American Magazine*.

No longer could we forecast the future from the past, he said, because now we had, in the Federal Reserve, "a unified banking system, the best security against those alternating periods of inflation and stringency which had made our business history a series of feasts and famines," plus business men who now knew "how to get the facts and interpret them." Yet this prediction, as America hovered on the brink, happily was qualified. For he pointed out that months ago he had drawn up a plan for the settlement of debts and reparations which "have been like dragging anchors to the great ship of international commerce." Under it, Germany would be assigned a reparations sum she could pay and "when it has been worked out, I believe we shall enter . . . the 'industrial renaissance.' " But then, alas, while he avoided advising the average man on his investments, "he cannot go far wrong if he relies on Progress . . . what I have called 'the industrial renaissance.' " An old friend had said, "How many bears do you know with residences on Fifth Avenue? I can recall none." However, a few brief years later, one of the few was to be B. M. Baruch.

Meanwhile the market soared and presently he sniffed signs and portents of the final crash, even as dogs and cats leapt skyward. Everybody was reaping riches from Wall Street, even Baruch's chosen literary and artistic playmates, who now were so busy watching the ticker they had no time to write or act. In mid-29 as the market bulged toward its bursting point, Arthur Krock, Alec Woollcott, Franklin P. Adams and Harpo Marx were week-ending with Baruch in Atlantic City, all happy to be with a sage who with one wise tip could make them rich. Timidly they fished for it.

"Do you know what I would do with my money?" said Baruch finally. There was a dead silence, except for the shooting galleries and peanut-whistles in the background. Then came a grotesque anti-climax. For, instead of a whisper about Kruger or Insull, he said, incredibly, "I'd put it in 4 per cent bonds."

Dig a hole and bury it? While others made millions! The old boy might have been good in his day, but now he was senile! When Black Friday came a few weeks later, as the ticker dropped hours behind under the load of selling orders, they understood.

Even before the market had made its final upward lunge, Baruch had made himself highly liquid. Did this skilled speculator presently go short? Does a ski champion crouch on a turn? Both operations are instinctive.

Alvin Johnson points out that Baruch is "essentially an economist with nerve . . . When he speculated, he assured himself of the basic realities. He bought when stocks or commodities were too low: he sold when they were too high. . . . If there had been more B.M.B.s there would have been no such skyrocketing as produced the boom . . . and the horrible crash that followed." Always Baruch has maintained that short-selling is useful, that bears are public benefactors. A market without them is like a country without a free press. There is no one to criticize inflated absurdities.

He considered his good friend, the notorious bear, Ben Smith, to be far more useful to the country than those fatuous titans of finance who had syphoned sucker money into the bull market with their rosy statements.

and F.D.R.

While the Republicans worried, Bernard Baruch kept what he had by the process of selling short just enough to balance his losses in things like Texas Gulf Sulphur which he wished to hold. Meanwhile as paper values vanished, Alaska Juneau, that bottomless gold mine into whose shaft he had previously shovelled more than three million, began to pay fat dividends, rising from the market's depths like a submerged castle of hard, gleaming metal, from an ebb-tide of fluttering paper securities.

While yesterday's optimists sweated, Baruch in those dark days of the crash could "live like a prince," as Alvin Johnson remembers. There was that night after an annual WIB reunion when he brought the boys and their guest of honor (John J. Pershing) to his Fifth Avenue mansion where they found (it was during prohibition) a perfect bar with a brass rail. The impressed General of the Armies, not knowing quite where he was, peered from the pinch bottles and Chianti flasks around the big mirror's base to the life-size, full-bosomed marble Venus Anadyomene who lolled in a sea shell at its top.

"I didn't know this place, Mr. Baruch. Do you think I could get a card?"

As the depression deepened, Baruch was occasionally consulted by President Herbert Hoover. ("We've been good friends since 1910," the ex-President remembers, "when we met in the mining business. I appreciate his sterling character.") With no prompting from President Hoover, but just to keep the Democratic Party's record straight, he persuaded his close friend, Senate leader Joe Robinson not to oppose confirmation of Chief Justice Hughes. He also worked hard for the passage of President Hoover's Reconstruction Finance Corporation in spite of his Democratic friends' misgivings— "Don't let that man pick your brains to get himself out of the hole he's in."

He also proposed some ideas of his own, favoring (before the Boston Chamber of Commerce in May of 1930) suspending the anti-trust laws to permit a "Supreme Court of Industry" which would allow "common sense cooperation among industrial units," thus preventing "our economic blessings from becoming unbearable burdens." Here was the yet unfertilized egg which soon hatched the Blue Eagle.

The recent boom and current downswing he felt had passed out of the realm of economic science and into that of mass psychology.

"You can't deal with a mad crowd," he insisted. "You can't tell when the herd will turn and trample you!" So he went along, from time to time selling short to protect himself.

His favorite reading was a reprinted classic, *Extraordinary Popular Delusions and the Madness of Crowds,* which described not only the seventeenth century witch-hunts and the Dutch tulip craze, but the speculative mania of the Mississippi Scheme and the South Sea Bubble, and he wrote for it a preface pointing out that even in past times people had wondered if declines would ever halt, but "They always did."

In June of 1932 his private railroad car stopped at Chicago where it disgorged a merry cast of characters as the Democrats were convening to nominate a candidate. Baruch's old WIB colleague Albert C. Ritchie was now Maryland's governor and favorite son. But true to his 1924 vow, Baruch had given no money or support to any candidate.

"Why should I?" he exploded to Hugh Johnson. "I don't want public office. I don't want anything from the party. I only want to serve it."

When Franklin D. Roosevelt was nominated, Baruch was consulted on the acceptance speech, in spite of the deep misgivings of Ray Moley, an early Roosevelt brain-truster, who in that period considered himself a dangerous radical, and so feared that the Democratic Party's lamentable poverty might force on its candidate Bernard Baruch's Wall Street and Big Business slant. Leftish Mr. Moley was overjoyed when this financial monster pronounced the speech "magnificent!"

During the campaign, Roosevelt headquarters was in a chronic state of fiscal crisis which on major occasions Bernard Baruch met almost singlehanded. They had practically nothing either for a campaign in the crucial state of Maine, or to buy network time for the golden Roosevelt voice, until Baruch either gave the cash or raised it. He also reassured Wall Street as to Governor Roosevelt's soundness on financial questions and helped Carter Glass prepare attacks on the "uncontrolled spending" of that reckless squanderer Herbert Hoover. Presently not only Baruch but his henchmen Herbert Swope and Hugh Johnson were definitely within the fringes of the Roosevelt Brain Trust. Its inner sanctum, however, was guarded jealously by Louis McHenry Howe, who constantly needled Roosevelt by recalling that, before his nomination, "Bernie wouldn't give us a nickel when we really needed it."

"But Baruch doesn't want anything," expostulated Senator Key Pittman.

"And he isn't going to get anything," said Howe firmly.

Mr. Howe succeeded in being right. While Baruch had declined Woodrow Wilson's offer to make him Secretary of the Treasury, he was given no chance to decline anything under the New Deal. Governor Roosevelt was nominated in 1932 only because William Randolph Hearst withdrew his candidate, John Nance Garner of Texas, and threw all his weight to Roosevelt. Mr. Hearst presently suggested to Governor Roosevelt via McAdoo that he would like Bernard Baruch to be named as Secretary of State.

But when, after November, the President-Elect began picking his cabinet, nothing came of this, nor of more persistent urgings that Baruch be named Secretary of the Treasury. This office went instead first to William H. Woodin, a neighboring Dutchess County squire, whose principal qualification for handling billions lay in his hobby of coin collecting, and later to Henry Morgenthau, Jr.

A few days before the Roosevelt inauguration and as the bank holiday was gathering momentum, Mr. Baruch gave at Johns Hopkins an address which would rank as a state paper.

Speaking of the self-reliance of the early colonists, this seventh-generation American pointed out that "the weak perished, the timid never came. Gregor Mendel, culling his sweet peas, used no more certain a method of selective breeding." Swinging hard against the tariff which "is now paralyzing the commerce of the world," he argued that "Thomas Jefferson stood for opposing principles . . . special privileges for none, equal opportunities for all. It was a rule to protect the weak from the aggression of the strong. But weakness wants something more. It wants something to lean on." Today "there is hardly a class which seems willing to stand on its own feet. Banks and railroads no less than farmers and workers . . . turn in their distress to Pennsylvania Avenue and almost never to Main Street. Everybody leans on government, blind to the fact that government by its very nature leans against everybody." Although "our sole remaining reliance is the federal credit, we . . . are now meditating a method to destroy it by one universal act of repudiation. It was in just such a maelstrom . . . that King Saul, in his confusion, went to Endor to consult the witch." And now "our modern witch-doctors appear and get credit for their incantations."

Meanwhile he had proposed to a Senate Committee a recovery program almost offensive in its simplicity and based on the premise that "we cannot oppose legislation to natural laws." He recommended that the government buy or rent sub-marginal farms to abolish crop surplus. It should firmly balance its ordinary budget, and put on a solid loan basis any money needed for relief, or to secure re-employment.

As for private corporations with bloated debts, let them go through the wringer, with revised bankruptcy laws which would allow "a quick and effective reorganization," the object being "to get people back to work again."

As for the incoming President, he was still confident, not because of the $53,000 he had given to his campaign, but because, in the inter-regnum period, he was being frequently consulted. "Apparently," he confided to a friend, "I am to be responsible for the economic side of this whole thing." But as it turned out, this burden was to be something short of crushing.

and F.D.R.

For some time, as a hedge against the clamors of Father Coughlin and the soft money agitators, he had been accumulating gold, withdrawing none from the Federal Treasury but importing some from abroad and getting his Alaska Juneau dividends not in paper dollars but in virgin gold bars from its quartz tunnels.

He was profoundly shocked when one of the first acts of the Roosevelt administration was to suspend gold payments, followed quickly by a law making illegal the possession of gold by private citizens. Promptly he turned in to the Treasury every ounce, receiving only the official pegged price in paper dollars, and making not one cent of profit. But where did this law leave our country?

Only yesterday its currency had been based on that sparkling yellow metal which has had value since the dawn of history. What was our money now? Long strips of water-marked paper, whose value lay only in the fact that it was also impregnated with red and blue silk threads, to insure that no one could print it in unlimited quantities except politicians, legally elected and properly sworn.

"Abandoning the gold standard is cheating!" he privately stormed. "The crowd has seized the seat of the government and it is trying to seize the wealth."

Publicly, however, he said nothing. At the new American President's suggestion, a World Economic Conference had been convened in London, with Ray

79

Moley, then the top Presidential favorite, presently arriving as his nuncio, and with Herbert Swope as an out-rider. Moley's White House duties were taken over by Baruch, who was increasingly embarrassed when reporters now referred to him as "Assistant President," since the President had privately remarked that "I don't mind if Bernie gives the impression that he writes all my speeches, but I do object to his claiming only the best ones."

There was, at this juncture, still a chance that America would return to gold which the more solvent European nations (France, Holland, Belgium and the Scandinavian countries) hoped desperately we would do. But new advisors, crowding around Roosevelt, were urging that paper inflation would boost domestic prices, so he wrote a statement chastising and in effect repudiating that Conference which originally he had called.

Baruch and Moley privately protested but Roosevelt, now afloat for a vacation aboard the cruiser *Indianapolis* with Louis Howe, Henry Morgenthau, Jr., and other idealists, did not listen.

"Don't leave your warm bed," Baruch had warned Moley on the eve of his London trip. "Somebody will be in it when you get back." Moley returned to find it had been expertly crowded by Felix Frankfurter, with the result that Tommie Corcoran, Ben Cohen and Rex Tugwell were smiling complacently back at him from the downy pillows of this ideological seraglio.

Yet Baruch men were, at this point, holding their own among the Happy Hot Dogs, for George Peek, his agricultural expert, was administering the AAA, while faithful Hugh Johnson was acting as goose-girl to the Blue Eagle.

Baruch himself still had the Presidential ear, but perhaps less frequently, for although Baruch listened patiently to the national planning schemes of the Happy Hot Dogs, in the hope of trimming them down to practicality, all too often he took issue with Roosevelt, who complained that "Bernie is very stubborn."

"Yes," snorted their mutual friend Senator Carter Glass, "especially on a proposition like two plus two equals four. Bernie can be dogmatic as hell about that."

"Am I supposed," mourned Baruch, "to yield for the sake of being pleasant, and say they could make six if the government insisted on it?"

It seemed so, and even the President's mother, Mrs. James Roosevelt, was disturbed. She trusted Bernard Baruch, and if the out-dated girlhood education of this dowager had been lacking in social vision, it was firmly grounded in arithmetic. Once she invited Baruch to Hyde Park. During the lunch her son was dutifully charming but excused himself early for in the next room he had "an important caller."

In the fall of 1933 Baruch, summoned by a Senate Committee, spoke up with embarrassing bluntness on the subject of our departure from gold. As for the effects of "this new attempt at boot-strap aviation" abroad (it had cheapened American goods to foreigners), he said, "this country has done some mad things in its foreign relations. It has wandered out among the hungry nations with its pockets bulging and its wits wandering—the International Fat Boy of All Time—and it has nearly ruined itself and a large part of the rest of the world by its actions."

And at home we were now "printing money which has no value behind it, and is money only because the government says it is. People who talk about gradually inflating, might as well talk about firing a gun off gradually. . . . We shall have set loose the avalanche of uncontrolled and uncontrollable inflation. . . . Money cannot go back to work in an atmosphere filled with the threat to destroy its value."

Meanwhile the Frankfurter boys (the pressure was slow and gentle) were quietly massaging both Ray Moley and Baruch out of the White House inner circle. They presently hinted that Baruch, via Hugh Johnson, was controlling NRA. Baruch had not urged Johnson for this post ("Roosevelt," he once snorted, "didn't ask me for Johnson—he took him!").

and F.D.R.

But when in 1934 Baruch sailed for an extended European vacation, it took the heat off his old friend. In London his other old friend, Winston Churchill, was politically out of favor as a hysterical war-monger who imagined that Germany, under this new fellow, Adolf Hitler, would re-arm. Strangely, Baruch agreed and came back talking stockpiles. Why didn't we start taking rubber and tin on our foreign debts? Then, if we were cut off—

But this could not happen. For, as every fair-haired young Marxist then knew, wars were caused solely by the greed of munitions makers for profit. Corporations cleverly arranged to have our sons sent to slaughter to increase dividends. Pursuing this theory the Nye Committee was preparing to de-bunk World War I, cheered on not only by the Communists, but Father Coughlin and Huey Long.

What about this big international banker Baruch? Hadn't he got his in war stocks? Why not dig into his wartime tax returns? Get him on the stand and Felix Frankfurter's alert Alger Hiss (The Nye Committee's investigator) would pull out all the answers.

So in early 1935 Baruch appeared with what records he had. To committee hints that he might have destroyed others, he could reply that while the Bureau of Internal Revenue had told him that "the original returns for 1918 and 1919 had been destroyed (by them) and my copies had not been sent back, they were supplying to me full copies of the reports made by field agents" and also proved that "never from the moment I was called to the government service did I have a dollar's worth of interest in any concern manufacturing munitions of war." The total picture showed Baruch's income during the war years had slumped, and for some years was even a loss.

This established, he tried to steer them down from fairy tales and back to the dull realities of war finance. Profiteering, he pointed out, was only one problem of war mobilization, which should insure that "each man, each business, everything and every dollar should bear its just proportion of the burden."

By the second day the committee was apologizing to its intended victim and, if the White House was neutrally silent, Jimmie Byrnes walked up to tell the committee not only of how Bernie had shipped the stenographers back to their mothers, but of the time when we needed to send a mission to England but had no appropriation, so Baruch had dug down into his own pocket for the $85,000, and had then refused to accept reimbursement.

Regardless of how Baruch stood at the White House, in the Senate Jimmie Byrnes, Pat Harrison, Joe Robinson and Key Pittman knew him well and would always go to bat, being considered by the waspish Frankfurter boys as a "Praetorian Guard" of

Senators who, because Baruch may have contributed to their campaigns, now "hang on his every word."

But it was definitely a Frankfurter year. First George Peek was out of AAA and soon Hugh Johnson was bringing his woes to Baruch, wishing plaintively that "I had your faculty for getting things done through charm," which reminded Baruch of a once-famous slugger, "but then somebody came along to teach him to box" and when "he began dancing around and delivering fairy taps, soon they carried him through the ropes feet-first. Go in there and be yourself, and not Bernie Baruch, nor J. Ham Lewis, nor Lord Chesterfield." With which Baruch left for Europe.

But came a day when Johnson was unexpectedly invited to the White House, and found waiting for him with the President his arch-enemies, Donald Richberg and Madame Perkins who "while they responded to my greeting, neither of them looked up." Then the ever-smiling President proposed that Johnson go abroad with "B. M. Baruch, Gerard Swope, anybody I wanted to take to study recovery in European countries." Sensing this as the sugary lipstick smeared over the kiss of death, Johnson suspiciously asked what would become of NRA. The President genially felt that this was "a detail."

Back at his hotel, the devoted Hugh Johnson "tried to call Bernie Baruch in Prague but could not reach him" and "never suffered more than I did in the next few hours before I wrote my letter of resignation."

When Baruch returned it was no better. The President was reported as "tired of that old Pooh-Bah" and the Frankfurter boys who, according to a self-census conducted by Tommie Corcoran, now numbered 250 in government, were firm in power, representing a complete triumph of the true, the beautiful and the good, over the dreary science of arithmetic.

"You don't have to burn down the barn to get rid of the rats," Baruch would snap, and only slowly did the suspicion grow that maybe some of them took a secret delight in the pink glow of flaming barns.

George Creel, Baruch's old friend from Wilson's times, chronicled the sad fact that "slowly but efficiently, inch by inch, the Palace Guard had eased him away from the seats of the mighty and over into the leafy solitudes of La Fayette Square," where from a park bench he now surveyed the White House and watched a torrent of alphabet soup swirl on into history.

The Happy Hot Dogs sneered that Baruch sat there vainly watching the White House flag to signal him in to lunch. This in part he confirmed. "I would crawl on my hands and knees to the White House," he said soberly, "if I thought it would do my country any good."

86

Failing this, anyone could consult him, but presently the word went out that to be seen with Baruch was politically contaminating. For who could be sure that common sense might not be catching? So faithful George Creel soon noted that he "had his bench to himself except for the pigeons and the squirrels." Once when Creel stopped to enquire "how the old sacroiliac was bearing up under the strain," he whispered impishly back that business was better. "Yesterday my opinions were asked by two park attendants and a WPA economist."

In June of 1936 he was called in (did they need money?) to read the Roosevelt speech accepting a second term nomination. But during the election Baruch's good friend George Peek took the stump for Landon, the Happy Hot Dogs insisting Peek was saying only what Baruch thought. And although in 1937 Baruch took no part in the fight against the President's plan to pack the Supreme Court, almost all his old Senate friends were lined up against it.

Again in Europe, "War is coming very soon," Churchill told him. "We will be in it and you [the U. S.] will be in it. You [Baruch] will be running the show over there, but I," Churchill added plaintively, "will be on the sidelines over here."

In part he was right, for Munich was not a year ahead, and Baruch returned to warn of "adamantine German nationalism" and to preach a two-ocean navy, stockpiles of strategic materials, air-power and tanks.

His old friend, Louis Johnson, Assistant Secretary of War, was gloomy. "Do you know that we have no machinery for making smokeless powder?"

"Why don't you buy some?"

"We have no appropriations."

"How much would the machinery cost?"

"Three million dollars."

"Go ahead and buy it. . . . Tell the manufacturers I will pay for it."

Yet somehow without Baruch Johnson got the money, although America was then in the mood to believe she could stay aloof from Europe by passing the Pittman Neutrality Bill, which embodied the "cash and carry" principle. Baruch dubiously felt that these laws "may or may not keep us from actual' fighting" since "what this act really does is to transfer from the Congress to the President the right to take steps that might lead to war." Our best protection lay in the fact that "this administration is building up our Navy to its greatest strength. It has accumulated an unprecedented war-chest in gold . . . it is in process of withdrawing from the terribly dangerous salient of the Philippine Islands" (a maneuver completed with Japanese assistance in 1942).

In 1938 he was still in the White House dog-house. The President, angry because his court-packing bill had failed in the Senate, attempted to purge those

88

Democrats (largely Southern) who had opposed him. When his purge backfired, the Happy Hot Dogs whispered that it was Baruch and other "reactionaries" who had helped finance these rebels.

Yet because printing-press money and pump-priming had failed to bring prosperity (the market had dived, unemployment had swelled), Baruch was now listened to most respectfully by the Senate Committee to Investigate Unemployment and Relief, with loyal Hugh Johnson (now a columnist) crisply observing that his old Chief's "effectiveness as a practical economist is suggested by his own magnificent solvency."

Baruch's keynote was that "if it became clear tomorrow that America has definitely chosen her traditional profits system, forces would be released that would rapidly hasten recovery and re-employment." Eloquently urging modification of the capital gains and undistributed profits taxes, he argued that we had reached the "law of diminishing returns. Weigh a horse too heavily in a handicap, and he will break down. . . . Man is like any other animal. If you place too great a burden on him, he will not work." And then, with great earnestness, "I have too much pride as a workman in anything that I may say or do, to make here a prejudiced statement. I would like to have the future justify me. I think it will."

Still fearing that a Pacific war would cut us off from rubber and tin, he finally got Henry Wallace to the point of trading off 600,000 bales of useless government surplus cotton for enough rubber tonnage to make 18,000,000 tires. And when Munich came that fall, he was not one who felt it had brought "peace in our time." Instead, swallowing his pride, he went to the White House to warn that Germany was plotting to split the Russians from the West, was even hatching a plot to conquer the Western Hemisphere. We must have an Atlantic-based fleet of 50,-000 long-range bombers. The President shrugged.

"The Nation is not ready."

"How," demanded military leaders, "can we spend a billion dollars a year usefully?"

They were to find out soon and when, in the spring of 1939, Hitler shattered Munich hopes by marching into Prague, Baruch and John Hancock (now with Lehman Brothers) went quietly down to Washington, Baruch as always offering his services and the two of them, who since 1920 had been lecturing at the War College, now curious to see what plans were ready for World War II.

As for Baruch's services, from Warm Springs came a rumored shake of the head and the remark, "Bernie's too old now."

"Baruch is too old," echoed the falsetto Palace Guard complacently, "and anyway it isn't his kind of a war," plus whispers that such an appointment would be vulnerable, as isolationists would say that "a Jew war-monger is getting us ready to fight."

But Hancock and Baruch found that Under-Secretaries of both Army and Navy thought the World War I industrial mobilization plan should be dusted off and brought up to date. Louis Johnson for the Army had appointed Ed Stettinius to the job when War Secretary Harry Woodring flounced home from a Panama trip, to announce primly that there would be no war plans in any administration he had anything to do with.

Through the summer Baruch and Hancock labored on at the Carlton, Baruch (who hates air-conditioning) trying vainly to plug the Carlton's cold-air ducts with their dirty shirts, and when this failed, fleeing to his park bench to warm up.

When France tottered in May of 1940 and Roosevelt promptly pledged America as "the great Arsenal of Democracy" Baruch's heart leapt high with hope, but when in the end the President appointed a powerless "advisory commission" called OPM, and with William Knudsen and Sidney Hillman as Siamese-twin co-chairmen, George Creel records that it took "two pulmotors to revive" Baruch.

Again he was under a political cloud for, although Mrs. Roosevelt liked him and frequently quoted him in the White House, his stock fell when the possibly over-loyal Hugh Johnson jumped the New Deal traces and came out not so much for Willkie as against Roosevelt, stumping the country with roars against White House vacillation and Palace Intrigue, and rousing suspicions that perhaps Old Iron Pants was really reading the discreet Baruch's mind, and shouting its contents into his microphones.

But Baruch now acquired in Washington a new disciple in Ferdinand Eberstadt, a brilliant young Wall Street executive, who confesses that "I was completely ignorant when I went to Washington in June of 1941 as Chairman of the Munitions Board," but quickly found that "Baruch's works were the great granite structures that covered the whole War production field," all of their present problems having been in the first World War "faced at least in embryo, and Baruch had studied them since." As for Eberstadt's associates, "some had paid lip-service to Baruch, but they hadn't studied his principles." As for Baruch, when he "found I was trying to put them into operation, he seemed pleased" (this could be an understatement).

That fall a House Committee, timidly tackling price control, was told bluntly by Baruch that "I do not believe in piecemeal price-fixing" but instead in "a ceiling over the whole price structure, including wages, rents and farm prices." He preached on his park bench the same tough doctrines to Leon Henderson, hoping, as George Creel chronicles, that "here at last was a two-fisted guy—a baritone, not a tenor."

Everybody listened (they always do) but the White House Bill which finally went through Congress did the exact opposite, a contraption with soft gums instead of teeth, which carefully exempted from politically unpopular control, both wages and farm prices.

"Of course, they couldn't be bothered with *good* advice," snorts loyal little Billy Rose, "so what happens? We lose I estimate a hundred billion smackers through inflation!" For, as Baruch had warned Congress before Pearl Harbor, "Except for human slaughter . . . inflation is the most destructive consequence of war. . . . Unless America has a low price structure when the war ends, we may win the war only to lose the peace."

So we drifted, the situation becoming more tense, and during the week in which Pearl Harbor was to fall, Baron Kurusu, special Japanese peace envoy, came secretly to the door of the man who, in distant Japan, they believed to be close to Roosevelt.

"Kurusu," Baruch remembers, "was very uneasy about the situation: war might break out at any time." So Baruch replied that even though America might at the moment be unready, did they seriously believe in Tokyo that, in the long pull, Japan could stand up against America?

Kurusu at least apparently did not, for now came

his suggestion: why could it not all be settled by America's arbitrating between Japan and China? And if this offer would come, not through ordinary diplomatic channels, but by a direct public appeal from President Roosevelt, over the heads of generals, admirals and diplomats, to the Emperor himself?

It might well have been, only at the White House they were very busy that week with other things until, just at dawn on Sunday, bombs began to explode on our Pacific fleet ("No!" was the President's first unbelieving comment) and America was at war.

Our War Department, which recently had been appalled at the prospect of a single billion, now stood eager to spend scores, which alarmed Baruch no less than had the bottlenecks, since one might well fear that the groping minds which had failed through random squandering to buy prosperity, would now fail to purchase victory. "Get rid of the idea that money is a force in itself," he insisted. "It's what you do with it that counts."

The White House Palace Guard had a further delicate problem in the fact that Winston Churchill, instead of being, as he had predicted, "on the sidelines," was now running England's war effort. Presently he arrived in Washington, rumbling uneasy enquiries as to where was his "old friend" of World War I, not understanding why that "strong, clear mind" which in 1918 by cable took those quick decisions, should now be feeding squirrels in La Fayette Park. It was most painful. So briefly that White House flag went up, and Baruch was summoned to a lunch which was, as George Creel mournfully recorded, only a "personal appearance," nothing more.

PART FOUR

Baruch and the Atom
(1946-1950)

From his bench and through the flapping pigeons Baruch was watching the creation of a swarm of war boards, each with limited and conflicting authority—OEM, OPM, OPA, BEW and finally the unbelievable SPAB which he pronounced "a faltering step forward and maybe backward." Even when the War Production Board was finally set up under Donald Nelson, Baruch at first feared it would again be only "coordination by conference" but presently conceded that Nelson's appointments were good, "Wilson, Eberstadt, Jeffers and Knollson have raised the whole standard" and soon they were frequent guests in his Carlton Hotel room.

John Hancock, who had served under Baruch in 1918, points out that even after the three wasted years preceding WPB, Nelson "came to the old Baruch pattern of centralized authority rather reluctantly. But he found you can't fight a war in a debating society."

Likewise brilliant Ferd Eberstadt, heading the Munitions Board, was now following Baruch's old World War I formula: "On one side of the table you put the people who make steel, and on the other those who need it, with the government in between. Then you must strike a bank balance. Because if you let contracts for more than can be produced, then you will have tanks without tracks and guns without barrels."

And because we now also had, as Baruch had predicted, cars without tires, not even enough rubber to mount our artillery, he was at last called to the White House and the rubber mess laid in his bony lap. If compared to WPB it was, as John Hancock says, a "sideline operation," at least it "took the heat off Roosevelt from those who were demanding Baruch." Hancock himself refused to go on the main board ("The New Dealers don't like me") which was composed of James B. Conant (Harvard) and Karl T. Compton (MIT) with the chairmanship to Baruch who immediately told Hancock it had to be a "hurry up job" and "you decide who studies what."

Since World War I was almost a quarter century back, John Hancock was one of the few surviving WIB veterans. But there was no need to change Baruch methods which now as then were, according to Hancock, that "the staff men take assignments and bring back reports. He exposes himself to the facts, asks for documentation and proof, and makes final decisions." Or as Baruch modestly remembers it, "Conant concentrated on processes and Compton on the amount-on-hand and compounding. I just added to the scenery."

Toward the end there was a final conference between the three on Baruch's La Fayette Square park bench, with Conant and Compton lashing at each other with molecular-chain formulae until Baruch finally interrupted:

"When you fellows get through talking Chinese, I believe we can go ahead and declare a dividend." This turned out to be gas-rationing and a 35-mile speed limit to save rubber, plus recapping and tire inspection, plus plants for making Buna S to be built in 1943 and to be turning out an annual 30,000 tons by 1944.

And when the three took this report to the White House, Baruch remembers that the President "took it fine . . . read it and issued a directive to put it into execution."

There was now strong pressure for a bigger job for Baruch and finally (years later it came out) the White House momentarily dangled before him Nelson's job as head of WPB. What then happened? "The President did not give me any reasons. It was never brought up again. He changed his mind, as he had a right to do."

Yet although many have noted that Baruch had developed a strong taste for lunching at the White House regularly, it did not lead him to truckle, and when his old friend, Jimmie Byrnes, was appointed Czar over all other Czars, with the title of Director of the Office of War Mobilization, Baruch accepted an appointment as advisor to this new *Shah in Shah* only on the understanding that the new body "is to be the *final* expression of the Commander-in-Chief and therefore it will *not* be by-passed or side-tracked," so that Jimmie Byrnes could "stop all this infernal *bickering.*"

The first assignment given by Byrnes to Baruch and John Hancock was the man-power problem. On our Atlantic coast there was hardly a surplus, but new war plants were being erected in the West where there was a more serious labor shortage, and consequently higher "take-home." Workers were scrambling to the West coast and manufacturers were even "stockpiling" labor—paying high wages for no work to men they might need.

The Baruch remedy was a labor budget. No new war contracts would go to regions already short of labor. Manufacturers were limited in the numbers they could hire; labor limited in its choice of jobs. And on the end of the report were two stingers: a sharp rebuke to "cost-plus" contracts which made possible labor-hoarding at public expense, plus the comment that "there are entirely too many agencies studying these problems, and not getting enough done."

Baruch's reputation was rising. "Don't say I'm a miracle man," he would protest to reporters. "I haven't got any rabbits I can pull out of my sleeve."

But in Baltimore a butcher without meat faced angry housewives: "Listen, ladies! Barney Baruch has just took a job in Washington and soon everything is going to be a lot better!" Yet Baruch liked best the comment of one of his Hobcaw colored maids who, when she heard the news, said reverently, "Jesus, prop him up!"

Washington now began to feel Baruch's value, and Jimmie Byrnes was glad to have Baruch and his team not solely because, as practical John Hancock puts it, "there would be no office budget or expenses" although Baruch at 72, and now known as the Man Who Can Solve Anything, was spending on public service at the rate of $200,000 of his own dollars per year (in the last quarter century it has cost him an estimated $2,500,000).

The newspapers never questioned Baruch's basic integrity nor his loyalty to America for, as John Hancock points out, "everyone knows Baruch is not out either for votes or [like the $1 a year men] for some private corporation." Baruch's strength in public life has been the fact that he wanted nothing for himself.

"Because what could you do for him?" demands adoring Billy Rose. "Get his name in the papers? Show him how to make a buck?" Weirdly enough Baruch never seemed busy. He would see a government official as early as 8:30 in his Carlton suite, but all day had plenty of time to joke with the cigar girl, effortlessly to handle a storm of telephone calls and minor visitors, and to chat with the same early-bird official as late as midnight.

"How can you take it?" one of these asked.

"As long as there's a German or a Jap left, and a pretty woman to look at, I can stand the pace."

Week-ends he was back in New York and although he had given up his big Kershaw racing stable, there was usually time to go to the races with Herb Swope although, what with more exciting diversions such as the war, his bets dropped to a "nominal" figure of $50 or so.

After rubber and man power, Jimmie Byrnes handed him "Industrial Demobilization," the knotty problem of pulling apart our war economy and gluing it back into a peace machine. It was at a time when Henry Wallace and his school were predicting that war's last gun would be followed instantly by a rush-tide boom of over-production, then by a gigantic slump, unemployment and hunger marches unless we moved quickly toward socialism and public works as our only guarantee of 60,000,000 jobs.

The Baruch-Hancock report, released in 1944, first recommended quick and uniform termination of war-contracts, so we should not "quibble the nation into a panic" by creating "unemployment by audit." The matter of selling surpluses should be "conducted in a goldfish bowl," selling in "small lots wherever possible, dividing and subdividing to the limit." And "let none feel that precious surpluses . . . of metal, raw materials, ships and airplanes will smother and engulf us: these are assets of tremendous value."

As for those gigantic public works, the Apostle of the Obvious pointed out that after the war billions would have to be spent on new homes, cars, clothing, pots, pans, vacuum cleaners, iceboxes. And with factories, railroads and airlines clamoring for new heavy equipment, where was the sense in setting up a Federal Works Program which would compete with these real needs?

There had been, he felt, "too much loose parroting of the slogan that if individual enterprise fails to provide jobs for everyone, it must be replaced by some of the other economic systems that are around." He pointed out that during the war our system had been pitted against Naziism, Fascism and Communism, and "has out-produced the world." Our only danger was that pressure groups might "turn that productive capacity into a battleground for their own selfish interests."

"You don't distribute wealth, you distribute poverty," he insisted and our nation's strength lay "not in what the government owns, but in what its people own. The sinews of production are not dollars; they are efforts."

For these reasons he advanced the shattering notion that a post-war depression is *not* inevitable because "handled with competence, our adjustment . . . is sure to be an adventure in prosperity." And then to reporter Henry Taylor, "If this program carries the scream of the American Eagle, it is because I feel that the old bird is in his own right and deserves first attention in the world aviary!"

The applause was still echoing when in April 1944 it was announced that the President had accepted an invitation to spend two weeks at Hobcaw Barony, to rest and regain strength. What did it mean, Baruch's old friends in the Senate wondered, as the two weeks stretched to four. Probably that Baruch at long last was forgiven for not passing the late Louis Howe's strict test of having been "for Roosevelt before [1932 in] Chicago." Yet in the Senate they hoped the visit might profoundly affect history, because "any man who talks to Baruch every day for four weeks will have an enormous admiration for him the rest of his life."

In that same spring, wishing to give a million to medicine in memory of old Dr. Simon Baruch, his son as always first sought expert advice which was (from Herbert Hoover), "Don't set up a new foundation. It will become a bureaucracy and waste your money. . . . Give it to existing institutions."

But to which? Who might know better than their mutual friend, Dr. Ray Lyman Wilbur, head of Le-land Stanford University, who presently headed the committee which allocated $400,000 to the Columbia Medical School, a quarter million each to the Medical Schools of New York University and of Virginia (from which Simon Baruch had graduated in 1862) with two more hundred thousand split up for special projects, fellowships and residencies, emphasis being put on research for the type of physical medicine which would benefit returning war cripples.

That year Baruch's relations with the White House were better than good. The following spring there was even talk of taking him to Yalta, but perhaps it was felt this was a job for sharp, alert young men like Ed Stettinius and Alger Hiss. Yet on the President's return there was another White House chat, which neither man realized would be final.

They talked of post-war problems, and Baruch proposed two great Councils, one in Europe for its reconstruction, one here at home to guide the peace, composed of key cabinet members and advisors. Roosevelt liked the idea, and what about Jimmie Byrnes as chairman, and also a small fact-finding staff which could be run maybe by Sam Rosenman. As for Baruch himself, "You're going to sit right next to Papa!"

In London when Baruch saw Sam Rosenman, he was also enthusiastic, and plans were moving. Then, on the news from Warm Springs, flags were suddenly lowered throughout the world. After this there was no more talk of councils. Overnight the balance of power had shifted from Hyde Park to Missouri.

Back from Europe now, Baruch in June cast pearls of wisdom before the Senate Military Affairs Committee. "What is done with Germany holds the key to whether Russia, Britain and the United States can continue to get along. . . . I have not thought in terms of a soft peace. I seek a sure peace. . . . I believe we can arrive at a full understanding with the Soviets—" only then, as always with Baruch, a shaft of hard realism breaks through the cloudy thinking of the day: "If it is not possible," he added, "the sooner we know it, the better."

That fall at Veterans' Administrator Omar Bradley's request, he prepared recommendations on veterans' problems: loans under the G.I. bill of rights should apply over 10 years, not two, and veterans opening new businesses should get an incentive tax cut of 25 per cent, to be applied against their loans.

And then as the dykes against inflation began to strain under demands both for higher wages and for huge American loans to Europe, he warned that "the race of selfishness is on" because more paper dollars circulating at home, due either to higher wages, foreign buying or lower taxes "will aggravate inflationary dangers unless our own production is rationed or until it increases."

and the Atom

Bernard Baruch's greatest contribution to world history was now approaching. In January 1946 the United Nations Assembly, then meeting in London, established the Atomic Energy Commission and the following month James Byrnes, American Secretary of State, privately told Baruch that he would be chairman of its American delegation.

Herbert Swope remembers that Baruch immediately told Byrnes and Truman, "I want my gang," so that was how it was—John Hancock, Herbert Swope, Ferdinand Eberstadt, Fred Searls, Jr. (a mining engineer), plus Richard C. Tolman, a California physicist.

A month before the public announcement John Hancock remembers he started his "usual scrapbook—read every scientific article so when the issue came up I would have the facts, be steeped in the problem."

But before they formally organized, Baruch took a farewell swing at economic matters, which were gently drifting to the dogs. In February President Truman had breezily favored an 18½ cent an hour increase in steel wages (it was an election year) and on March 26th Baruch was prophetically telling the House Currency and Banking Committee that "this will be followed by increases all along the line, no matter what anyone thinks to the contrary. Call it a bulge, but it is really a break, and a grave one. This was inflationary! . . . the price structure is now out of gear . . . a race of selfishness is in motion."

He begged them to "stop increasing the money supply," to "stop bunking the public by saying wage increases can be granted without increase in price levels" and to reconsider the six billion dollar tax cut they had made "for the purpose, it was said, of stimulating business, which already has orders it will take years to fill" because "I see at least 5 or 7 more years [the date was early 1946] of unending demand. How long that will last will depend on the wisdom we show. . . . We must stop treading this economic primrose path." The customary Baruch formula got its time-honored response: most respectfully they listened, and then did the opposite.

So now he was back with the atom. When on his New York park bench, Baruch first outlined his hopes for world atomic energy control to Ferd Eberstadt, the younger man (still old enough as a young lawyer to have been in 1919 with Baruch in Paris) said, "Boss, you've done great things, but you're now on the verge of the greatest. Because you're offering the world one of the most elevated programs ever given mankind! One which, if followed, not only can solve the atom, but the entire problem of war!"

With such aspirations they started, "prepared," Eberstadt remembers, "to make any compromises which did not affect the basic principle of free inspection and full control."

Only quickly the question came up, "To whom do we report?"

John Hancock thought the Secretary of State.

But Herbert Swope objected that the State Department was "already for the Acheson-Lilienthal report, and we're going far beyond that! Also our report might get reviewed by some 'expert' on Kamchatka." So Baruch told Jimmie Byrnes that, when it was finished, "we want to take it to the President because, since you're busy, I'd have to do what they tell me. And I'm too old to be a Western Union messenger." So it was agreed.

But their immediate problem was the Acheson-Lilienthal report, which Baruch's team studied, and which ended in what Herbert Swope delicately characterizes as "a set of pious platitudes. Like the Kellogg-Briand treaties, there was no provision in case a signatory was a violator." So a meeting with Dean Acheson was scheduled in Blair House in Washington and "the boys decided I [Swope] was to ask the hot questions, and then later Baruch would say, 'Oh, hell, I'll quiet Swope. Don't worry about him.'"

So finally came Swope's hot question: "Mr. Acheson, what *real* provision is there for inspection? What are you going to do if they *don't* behave?"

They then remember that the wounded Acheson, turning to Baruch, said: "Is this your question?"

111

They recall that Baruch gently nodded. And that Acheson then said:

"I suggest it be left to juridical interpretation."

So now Herbert Swope, with his legendary velvet-tipped tact which can be compared only to that of a run-away San Francisco cable car, observed that juridical interpretation was "absolutely meaningless to me!"

In response Dean Acheson explained that, well, in diplomacy these situations arise, not often, of course, but should it happen, then we could meet them and improvise.

Mr. Swope now wondered, "Is this the way you think matters of great importance should be treated?" Dean Acheson thoughtfully decided that on the whole perhaps it was, at which point it became clear to Baruch's team that there could not be a full meeting of minds with the State Department on its Acheson-Lilienthal report.

So they came back to New York, where they had a floor in the Empire State Building. John Hancock was in general charge, Baruch and Swope worked on the British, Searls on the Canadians and Searls plus Eberstadt on the French. They all argued that no sound agreement was possible without real inspection plus swift punishment for violators.

With the scientists they had help both from their physicist, Tolman, and from Major General Thomas F.

112

Farrell, who during the war had been Grove's alternate on the Manhattan Project, sharing with him (and him alone) all the top secrets. Army security would not let them fly in the same plane, lest one crash kill the only two men who knew the whole bomb recipe.

Swope remembers that the scientists were at first "very hoity-toity," talking grandly of the "sanctity and illimitability" of science, on which "none of us could dare to put boundaries" because "we must carry it through any limits it takes us." So then Swope had to be brutally frank first with Harold Ure, and next day with Robert Oppenheimer. Eberstadt noticed that when the scientists found Baruch was "a strong, capable man who could not be mystified with jargon, he had them eating out of his hand."

The French had ornamented their delegation by two men who, according to Eberstadt, "were well known even by the French delegation to be Communists," but when Baruch refused to deal with Joliot-Curie they presently repacked for Paris, and the man they left behind (the Count de la Rose) was a "wonderful guy."

The Russian opposite number to Fred Searls (a crack engineer with Neumont Mining whom Baruch had known since 1928) was Soviet mining expert Prof. S. P. Alexandrov, whom Searls had met when both witnessed our atomic test at Bikini lagoon. Alexandrov spent some time in America before the war, and was familiar with all our mines—"knew all about the Carnotite deposits in Southern Colorado," Searls remembers. He had come to like Alexandrov, whom he characterizes as "able, well-informed, but I thought he was scared to death of his superiors."

There was even a moment when Searls hoped he had a "half-way agreement" with Alexandrov to list world uranium reserves as the report of the World Geological Congress lists world coal deposits. When Searls showed Alexandrov a copy of this coal report, he seemed greatly interested. It would have been one real step toward inspection, but the next day Alexandrov's enthusiasm had cooled.

Meanwhile Ferd Eberstadt, digging back into history, had found that in 1928 Soviet Foreign Minister Maxim Litvinov had suggested to the stronger nations in Geneva a disarmament idea which was "substantially our proposals." Why were ours rejected now? Were they offered in 1928 because Russia had then been weak? "You couldn't yet be sure," says Eberstadt. "Suppose we had entered these atom meetings without preparation, and then the Russians had made our proposals, would we have accepted immediately?"

The trouble was that after a look at the American proposals as presented by Baruch on June 14,* the Russians said, "The result of this plan is to establish more firmly the American monopoly," and John Hancock points out that "they said it so quickly we knew

* See Appendix A, page 133.

114

it had not had time to be considered in Moscow."

But as the days went by Gromyko, who would talk only of abolition, repeated monotonously, "This is a terrible weapon."

"Yes," the Americans would answer, "the bomb *had* been used against women and children, but that is modern war. Now it can be a deterrent to aggression."

But always Gromyko would come back to his "women and children" and shrewd old John Hancock "never knew how sincere he was. Their diplomats are trained in debate, try to win it by any method," and this was neatly packaged for public consumption. It soon became clear to Hancock that the Russians either (1) did not understand our plan, or (2) before rejecting it, they were scouting for all the technical information they could pry or coax out of us. In July Gromyko announced to the American delegation that their own public opinion did not support the Baruch plan. How could Gromyko be so smugly sure?

"We did not then know," confesses John Hancock, "that Henry Wallace had already written his letter [made public only in September, and denouncing the Baruch plan] to President Truman."

Negotiations had started in June and Ferd Eberstadt presided over the July meeting. "Now I've spent a lifetime in trading," this direct Wall Street mind points out, "and I can tell whether a man is really out to do business and make a sale, or whether he is on a fishing trip for information. I felt their questions were disingenuous. A sincere man will say 'What do you mean by that?' or 'How will we work that out?' instead of just shouting 'It is wrong!'

"In August I decided they were publicly trying to put us on the spot, privately fishing for information, but didn't want a real agreement. So I went to Baruch and said,

" 'Boss, we've got a short sale here.'

" 'Why do you think so?' he asked. So I told him. Then he said,

" 'Maybe you're right. But still we have to keep on.'

" 'Why?' I asked. Then he quoted from the Declaration of Independence, that thing about how although we 'hold these truths to be self-evident,' nevertheless 'a decent respect for the opinions of mankind—' and so forth. 'It isn't enough that we know they're insincere,' Baruch told me. 'We must keep on trying until it becomes just as clear to all the world as it is now to you.' "

They had a further clue to Soviet motives. John Hancock, who presided over the American delegation in Baruch's absence, remembers that Soviet scientist Alexandrov, on his way back as our guest at the Bikini tests, had told Honolulu reporters the Soviet Union would have the atomic bomb in "a measurable time." But in New York at meetings of the technical committee, Alexandrov "spent two weeks badgering our scientists for information until Tolman finally called me over to stop it."

"I was surprised by your West Coast statement," Hancock told Alexandrov. "What do you mean by 'measurable'?"

"That means soon."

"Doctor, I don't believe you."

"Why, may I ask you?"

"If you were near a bomb now, you wouldn't be devilling Tolman with those questions in the secret session."

Hancock had touched Soviet pride. Two days later, "I want to make it very clear," Gromyko loftily told the United Nations Assembly, "that Russia wants no information."

As for Gromyko in general, Eberstadt found him "a very competent man who dominated his Soviet bloc. While we could see he wasn't making his own decisions in the sense that Baruch was, he was still as free as were many of the other foreign delegates. In open meetings he was brusque and abrupt, as the Soviets think a Communist diplomat should appear to be. Outside them while he was always reserved, he was polite and gentlemanly. At the cocktail parties each group gave, the Russians kept to agreeable small talk. Gromyko is not only witty, but a master of the niceties of English. Once when the translator said,

" 'Mr. Gromyko says he is surprised,' Gromyko interrupted.

" 'I said I was amazed,' he insisted."

Baruch got along very well with Gromyko, who at one point suggested that he go to see Stalin. "But," said Swope, "we thought Baruch should have the permission of the President."

The biggest public crisis of the negotiations came in the early fall of 1946, when Baruch and his team had gone to Washington to give the President a "progress report" and at this moment Henry Wallace's July letter to Truman hit the headlines. It was in substance a defense of the Soviet atom position, based on a misrepresentation of America's proposals.

In the White House they agreed that first Wallace would be asked to retract but that if he did not, Truman would repudiate him (which subsequently he did, whereupon Wallace resigned from the Cabinet).

"I had liked Wallace during the war," says Eberstadt, "and when I saw he had put his name to this letter, I hoped he was misinformed. But after our interview, I saw that wasn't all. He had in addition seen an opportunity to exploit, and he couldn't resist. I saw a great deterioration in him."

It was a crucial meeting held in Baruch's room, with "Baruch trying to meet Wallace's views," as Hancock remembers it. "Here we were with Americans already confused and this letter making them more so. I carried the brunt of it, with Eberstadt cutting in." Wallace had arrived with only one apostle, a professor of sociology from his Commerce Department, Philip Hauser, now Acting Chief of Census, but Herb Swope remembers that, although Hauser was then sincerely trying to help Wallace, "I never saw a man act more cleanly."

"Where was I wrong?" asked Wallace.

"Mr. Wallace," said John Hancock, "here's what you said, and here's what the record is." But then Hancock felt that Wallace got "slippery as hell."

" 'I have a right to write the President,' " Wallace would answer.

" 'You have no right to write these things,' " Hancock told him, " 'when in five minutes on the phone with either Baruch or me, you could have been set right.' "

Finally Wallace "seemed to agree," says Herbert Swope, "that a correction should be prepared, and said, 'I will designate Hauser.' And Baruch said, 'We will designate Swope.' Hauser and I reached a complete agreement on the retraction, but then we couldn't find Wallace." Saturday he had been in Chicago, Sunday he had disappeared. Then finally Hauser called to say that Wallace "was gagging at certain things," and when they got Wallace on the phone, "I found him obdurate and so did Eberstadt."

"He told us," says John Hancock, "that his 'advisors' wouldn't let him eat crow. We told him crow wasn't a tasty dish, but that in the interests of the truth and the country, he'd better nibble a little."

"Finally," says Swope, "I said, 'Let's print the whole God damned thing,' and Baruch agreed." So presently he went to work with Swope who was, as Eberstadt points out, "our polish man on style and public relations."

Next morning Baruch released a statement lashing Wallace for refusing to correct the "errors," calling his letter to Truman either "misinformation or complete distortion," adding tartly that "You have no monopoly on the desire for peace" to the search for which "I have given 30 years of my life" and, in conclusion, "Everyone," wrote Baruch, "has a right to his opinions. But no man has a right to circulate errors."

"I've seen blockbusters," Jimmie Byrnes gleefully wired Baruch, "but nothing so complete!"

Eberstadt remembers that "October 13th was our day of decision. Herb Swope and I saw eye to eye. We wanted to bring this whole atomic matter to a final vote in the United Nations Assembly, which was about to meet.

"Some of our own group then wanted to temporize, and we also knew it would be painful for Atomic Commission members from some other countries which were under the Russian guns to stand up and be counted, even though privately they shared our views."

So then the Americans went to work, both on these shaky foreign delegates and on the document's final draft, which "on December 4th we put before the Committee," says Eberstadt, "telling them, 'Now here's what you're going to have to vote on,' " and on December 5th Bernard Baruch himself rose to address the assembled United Nations Atomic Energy Commission.*

"I beg you to remember," he pleaded, "that to delay may be to die. I beg you to believe that the United States seeks no special advantage." The basic proposals were:

(1) An international authority to develop atomic energy for social gain, and prevent the manufacture of bombs for war.

(2) The right of free and full international inspection to insure this.

(3) Punishment of violators unhampered by any veto.

"We welcome cooperation," concluded Baruch, "but we stand upon our basic principles, even if we stand alone. We shall not be satisfied with pious protestations, lulling the people into a false sense of security. We aim at an effective plan . . . will accept nothing less."

* See Appendix B, page 146.

121

And a few days later, accepting a Freedom House Award, he said, "The Soviets protest that inspection violates national sovereignty. Better that than international disaster. . . . America asks nothing she is not willing to give."

But all of America was not yet sure. The Foreign Policy Association, meeting in New York, wanted the Baruch plan explained and, according to Eberstadt,

"Baruch sent Herb Swope to give them a spiel. Then during the question period, some one got up and said that these proposals were all very nice, but what would we do if the Russians didn't agree?

" 'There will be no agreement,' Swope told them, and in a matter of hours we got a hot protest from the State Department for being rude to the Russians. But when they checked the stenographic record, Swope was okay."

The plan was now before the delegates, and Herbert Swope remembers that on the first morning The Right Hon. Sir Alexander Cadogan, P.C., C.M.G., K.C.B., came over to him:

"Herbert, this is very embarrassing. I understand your Chief believes we are going to support this thing in its entirety."

"Yes," said Swope.

"I don't know," said Cadogan. "This is very serious."

"I'll go get the boss."

When Baruch came over, Cadogan said, "Chief, this is most embarrassing. Do you expect us to support the entire American proposals?"

Whereupon Swope remembers that Baruch "drew himself up to his complete 6 feet 4 and said, 'I am holding you to your commitment!'

"Then Cadogan said, 'I have no right to commit the British Empire.'

"But Baruch answered, 'In my book you have.'"

Later Swope, pinioning another British knight, delicately asked, "what all this backing and filling meant. And he said, 'We know you have the bomb, but the Russians have the guided missiles.'"

Gradually the delegates from Western Europe took courage, but John Hancock remembers that, although "we were hoping to drive the Russians into a corner where they would have to define their position, as the year-end approached, Baruch saw no chance of an agreement with them. Because, with the confused situation in America they could dawdle"—it was unthinkable that a bomb would be dropped—"so they had nothing to lose by turning us down."

"The final vote," says Eberstadt, "came on December 30th, and it was very hard for some of the foreign delegates whose countries were under the Russian guns or within reach of the Red Air Force. But in the end they all stood up and were counted with us —except the Russians and the Poles."

"We made our final report on the last day of 1946," says John Hancock, going down to Washington to tell Jimmie Byrnes, who was also preparing to retire. Jimmie was concerned because he had got us into this job, and wouldn't be there to see us out. He didn't want to leave us flapping under someone else."

"It was Eberstadt," says Herbert Swope, "who was responsible for our resigning. 'We have nothing else to do but re-hash,' he pointed out. 'We have made magnanimous proposals. Now we should get out while the getting is good.'"

Eberstadt feels this was wise because "The Old Man isn't interested in agreements if they are unsound. Reaching one with the Russians is very easy —you need only consent to what they want. The problem is whether this would be better than our present position, which of course it isn't." And as for today, "We are now at a stage where the Nervous Nellies can make trouble. Because a politician always likes to come smiling back with an agreement, which he can say is 'peace in our time.'"

But to date there is no sign of this, for President Truman, despite later painful differences with Baruch, has so far stood firmly on his atomic offer.

"I am for the American proposals," he said, in laying the United Nations cornerstone, "until we get something better." Which so far we have not.

Mr. Baruch's differences with President Truman

began after the convention of 1948 with a cloud smaller than a man's hand. Washington heard rumors that he was contributing, as usual, to the Senatorial campaigns of old friends, although as yet he had in this election done little for the National ticket. Truman also remembered that the late President Roosevelt had just after the war appointed Baruch's brother, Herman, as Ambassador to Holland, a post which he still held.

Whereupon Truman, possibly at the instance of his fund-raisers, wrote Baruch, asking if he would serve on the National Democratic Finance Committee. At this point both Gallup and Roper polls unanimously were predicting Truman's defeat.

Baruch replied courteously that it was his lifelong practice (the record completely bears him out) never to serve on committees. But the irritated (and presumably out-going) President now sat down to write Baruch a crisp note to the effect that Baruch had had many favors, and Truman was sorry to find that when the going was rough, Baruch wasn't willing to reciprocate.

Nor was this all. Baruch's birthday (August 19th) was approaching. On this day he customarily gets, from any Democratic President, a telegraphed greeting. None came on this one but instead, on that happy day, a terse White House announcement that Brother Herman had been suddenly fired from his post in

Holland. Shortly before the election one columnist published an interview, which Baruch quickly pointed out was unauthorized. As reported by the columnist (and denied by Baruch) he gave the gist of the President's letter and then quoted Baruch as observing: "I did not reply at all. . . . Nor did I make any overtures to him, and I shall not. He is a rude, ignorant, uncouth man. Well, you newspapermen fell for him when he came in. . . . I didn't fall for him. I knew him too well."

On the election's eve he refused to comment on either Truman or his platform—"My views regarding the issues have been expressed over and over again."

A sub-zero coolness now exists between our Democratic President and his party's Elder Statesman. In a speech (June 1949 before the Armed Forces Industrial College) Mr. Baruch, criticizing our failure to adopt a plan for total mobilization, referred to the administration's "vacillation and neglect." This produced an immediate collision between iceberg and glacier, with flying chips of cracked ice.

"Mr. Baruch," replied the White House iceberg, "has been misinformed."

"I have not been misinformed," retorted the glacier. "The President has been misinformed."

In foreign affairs Mr. Baruch has been even more prophetically critical. Although his sharp eye is quick to spot pivotal European problems ("Great Britain has to get rid of its overhanging block of sterling debt") yet he has never favored the indiscriminate shovelling out of foreign aid, feeling for instance that the British also are "spending so much time nationalizing and socializing" that they are not "using their energies in developing their country for production."

In general he feels that because "this country is not strong enough to hold up the rest of the world indefinitely," all our foreign commitments "should now be re-examined." If at some given point we can break a deadlock, let us "pour it on" but in places where "no decision is possible, let us cut expenditures, and insist that these nations do more for themselves. Such a policy may provide rude awakenings for governments now content to coast on American aid." And as for the Marshall plan, early he warned the Senate that it would be "meaningless," unless backed up by "a firm American promise to go to war in the event of aggression," a statement he does not make lightly because "I would crawl on my hands and knees to the West Coast to keep the young men of the world from another war!"

As for our internal situation, he fears most of all inflation, brought about through a weakening of the nation's moral fibre. "There is too much emphasis on the alleged need for *more* purchasing power. What the country needs is *stable* purchasing power." And if we were piously shocked when overnight the Soviet

government slashed the ruble to a tenth of its value,
our own government has since been "steadily lessen-
ing the value of all savings, pensions and the like"
and if "savings are to be devalued by printing more
money in this incessant scramble for higher wages,
higher prices, higher profits and higher pensions,"
then "the moral basis of society will be destroyed"
and finally all will become "dependent on the Mother
State, but upon whom is the Mother State to lean?"

Inflation, he hammers home, is only superficially
"a problem in economics and money" but at bottom
"a matter of national character" for it is the result of
"each segment of society putting its own selfish interest ahead of the national interest." Looking back,
he puts an accusing finger on the Price Control Law
of 1942 (he had opposed it) which had "let wages
run free and farm prices rise" in spite of his warn-
ings and because it was politically popular. "That
law," he points out, "legalized inflation."

Then in midsummer of 1950 our government,
which had dreamily watched while Communist arms
engulfed most of Asia's mainland, inexplicably gagged
when they moved into South Korea and, in a quixotic
backward-flip of foreign policy, suddenly shoved into
this military booby-trap three divisions of badly trained
and poorly equipped young draftees from Japan.

As 60-ton Soviet tanks nosed the fragments of this

pathetic force back toward Pusan, Mr. Baruch, testifying as of yore before the Senate Banking Committee, again branded President Truman's timid "step by step" economic measures as "inadequate," proposed instead rationing, price-, wage-, and rent-controls. Compared to the start of World War II, "militarily, economically and spiritually we are worse off," he felt. "We can always make money," he insisted, "but we can't get our liberties back."

A closer look now at this wind-blown, beady-eyed old eagle today in his eightieth year. His fortune, which guesses once put as high as 25 million, has largely (and quietly) been given away, but "right up to the day they put the coffin lid on me," he says with a grin, "I'll always have a dollar more than I need."

This even allowed for such an occasion as the thousands which went (you would never learn this from him) to one of the late President's children, bewildered and in financial difficulties. Perhaps he remembered those days when, a humble petitioner on that La Fayette Park bench, he was always received with high graciousness by Mrs. Roosevelt ("She's a brave woman. I don't know anybody I'd rather go lion-hunting with").

In his grey-carpeted Fifth Avenue apartment overlooking his park bench there is the dull glint of the English antique furniture and the delicate hand-hammered George II silver collected by Annie Griffen

Baruch (she died in 1938). His present entourage consists of Miss Mary Boyle (his secretary since 1904) and Miss Elizabeth Navarro, a graduate nurse hand-picked for him several years ago by adoring Billy Rose. She jokes with him, picks lint off the lapels of his cutaway, restores his hearing-aid with fresh batteries ("My main job is stopping him from eating peanuts, and carrying his money for him").

He seldom accepts invitations, partly because "unless I dine at 7:30 sharp, I get cross and am poor company" and partly because he dislikes both opinionated bores and people with prying questions. In such crises his hearing aid (equipped with a secret cut-off) suddenly goes dead. Of one prominent politician he remarks with a grin, "I have heard nothing he has said to me since 1935."

Against any interviewer's questions which he considers improper, he has a stratagem which once wrung from the lyre of a lyrical *Fortune* writer an agonized twang when that baffled bard bitterly sang that "Baruch, squid-like, envelops himself in a dark cloud of self-revelation. The more he talks about himself, the more he obscures himself."

As for the Faith of his Fathers, in any era other than that of Adolf Hitler, he would have devoted no more time to considering the special problems of Jews than the late Calvin Coolidge devoted to those of Congregationalists. From boyhood Bernard Baruch has considered himself first an American, secondly a Southerner, thirdly a Confederate Democrat and lastly a Jew, this descending scale being a rough measure of the relative strength of his loyalties.

Yet, speaking from his heart and to his own people in his homeland (and this is not Tel Aviv, but Camden, South Carolina), he confessed last year: "I have had intolerance practiced against me and mine all my life. But I have never permitted it to rouse in me envy, jealousy or hatred, or to weaken in the slightest my faith in our form of government, its Constitution and its institutions."

Its effect instead may well have been to spur him to set an example of high service, not to the narrow interests of Jews, but to all his fellow-Americans, an example of broad and selfless patriotism perhaps unequalled since that other proud and brilliant Sephardic aristocrat, Benjamin Disraeli, became Prime Minister of Great Britain, to place upon the silvering head of England's little queen the golden diadem of that far-flung Empire upon which the Sun Never Sat, until a less-far-sighted generation of drab Socialist statesmen started dribbling it away.

Since Bernard Baruch's three children have as yet given him no grandchildren, our Republic is the adored child which at eighty he now dandles on his knee, alternately spanking it with sound criticism and spoiling it with praise.

131

Sometimes, looking at the world from the perspective of these four-score years, strange new trends disturb him and he fears we are entering a period when civilization is on the downgrade like the time in the Third Century when Roman civilization lost faith in itself, and the masses from Central Asia went on the trek. At such moments he considers abandoning the rule of a lifetime to stump the country, making a last-ditch fight.

But his hope is that our youth will regain the rugged, self-confident faith of his own boyhood, and this is why the Man Who Never Seems Busy can find time out from advising Premiers and Presidents to answer the request of a little midwestern high school and, in dedicating their year-book, to remind the children that "the Ten Commandments and the Sermon on the Mount are still our best guides. And remember that this government is the best in the world. Improve it, but guard it well, and don't lean too heavily on it. You can and must do for yourself," says the tall man who, in all of these eighty years, has proudly stood alone.

APPENDIX A

United States Atomic Energy Proposals

PRESENTED TO THE UNITED NATIONS ATOMIC ENERGY COMMISSION BY BERNARD M. BARUCH, THE UNITED STATES REPRESENTATIVE, JUNE 14, 1946

My Fellow Members of the United Nations Atomic Energy Commission, and My Fellow Citizens of the World:

We are here to make a choice between the quick and the dead. That is our business.

Behind the black portent of the new atomic age lies a hope which, seized upon with faith, can work our salvation. If we fail, then we have damned every man to be the slave of Fear. Let us not deceive ourselves: We must elect World Peace or World Destruction.

Science has torn from nature a secret so vast in its potentialities that our minds cower from the terror it creates. Yet terror is not enough to inhibit the use of the atomic bomb. The terror created by weapons has never stopped man from employing them. For each new weapon a defense has been produced, in time. But now we face a condition in which adequate defense does not exist.

Science, which gave us this dread power, shows that it *can* be made a giant help to humanity, but science does *not* show us how to prevent its baleful use. So we have been appointed to obviate that peril by finding a meeting of the minds and the hearts of our peoples. Only in the will of mankind lies the answer.

It is to express this will and make it effective that we have been assembled. We must provide the mechanism to assure that atomic energy is used for peaceful purposes and preclude its use in war. To that end, we must provide immediate, swift, and sure punishment of those who violate the agreements that are reached by the nations. Penalization is essential if peace is to be more than a feverish interlude between wars. And, too, the United Nations can prescribe individual responsibility and punishment on the principles applied at Nürnberg by the Union of Soviet Socialist Republics, the United Kingdom, France, and the United States—a formula certain to benefit the world's future.

In this crisis, we represent not only our governments but, in a larger way, we represent the peoples of the world. We must remember that the peoples do not belong to the governments but that the governments belong to the peoples. We must answer their demands; we must answer the world's longing for peace and security.

In that desire the United States shares ardently and hopefully. The search of science for the absolute weapon has reached fruition in this country. But she stands ready to proscribe and destroy this instrument—to lift its use from death to life—if the world will join in a pact to that end.

In our success lies the promise of a new life, freed from the heart-stopping fears that now beset the world. The beginning of victory for the great ideals for which millions have bled and died lies in building a workable plan. Now we approach fulfilment of the aspirations of mankind. At the end of the road lies the fairer, better, surer life we crave and mean to have.

Only by a lasting peace are liberties and democracies strengthened and deepened. War is their enemy. And it will not do to believe that any of us can escape war's devastation. Victor, vanquished, and neutrals alike are affected physically, economically, and morally.

Against the degradation of war we can erect a safeguard. That is the guerdon for which we reach. Within the scope of the formula we outline here there will be found, to those who seek it, the essential elements of our purpose. Others will see only emptiness. Each of us carries his own mirror in which is reflected hope—or determined desperation—courage or cowardice.

There is a famine throughout the world today. It starves men's bodies. But there is a greater famine—the hunger of men's spirit. That starvation can be cured by the conquest of fear, and the substitution of hope, from which springs faith—faith in each other, faith that we want to work together toward salvation, and determination that those who threaten the peace and safety shall be punished.

The peoples of these democracies gathered here have a particular concern with our answer, for their peoples hate war. They will have a heavy exaction to make of those who fail to provide an escape. They are not afraid of an internationalism that protects; they are unwilling to be fobbed off by mouthings about narrow sovereignty, which is today's phrase for yesterday's isolation.

The basis of a sound foreign policy, in this new age, for all the nations here gathered, is that anything that happens, no matter where or how, which menaces the peace of the world, or the economic stability, concerns each and all of us.

That, roughly, may be said to be the central theme of the United Nations. It is with that thought we begin consideration of the most important subject that can engage mankind—life itself.

Let there be no quibbling about the duty and the responsibility of this group and of the governments we represent. I was moved, in the afternoon of my life, to add my effort to gain the world's quest, by the broad mandate under which we were created. The resolution of the General Assembly, passed January 24, 1946, in London, reads:

Section V. Terms of Reference of the Commission

The Commission shall proceed with the utmost despatch and enquire into all phases of the problem, and make such recommendations from time to time with respect to

135

them as it finds possible. In particular the Commission shall make specific proposals:

(*a*) For extending between all nations the exchange of basic scientific information for peaceful ends;

(*b*) For control of atomic energy to the extent necessary to ensure its use only for peaceful purposes;

(*c*) For the elimination from national armaments of atomic weapons and of all other major weapons adaptable to mass destruction;

(*d*) For effective safeguards by way of inspection and other means to protect complying States against the hazards of violations and evasions.

The work of the Commission should proceed by separate stages, the successful completion of each of which will develop the necessary confidence of the world before the next stage is undertaken. . . . [1]

Our mandate rests, in text and in spirit, upon the outcome of the Conference in Moscow of Messrs. Molotov of the Union of Soviet Socialist Republics, Bevin of the United Kingdom, and Byrnes of the United States of America. The three Foreign Ministers on December 27, 1945, proposed the establishment of this body.[2]

Their action was animated by a preceding conference in Washington on November 15, 1945, when the President of the United States, associated with Mr. Attlee, Prime Minister of the United Kingdom, and Mr. Mackenzie King, Prime Minister of Canada, stated that international control of the whole field of atomic energy was immediately essential. They proposed the formation of this body. In examining that source, the Agreed Declaration, it will be found that the fathers of the concept recognized the final means of world salvation—the abolition of war. Solemnly they wrote:

We are aware that the only complete protection for the civilized world from the destructive use of scientific knowl-

[1] *Department of State Bulletin*, Feb. 10, 1946, p. 198.
[2] *Department of State Bulletin*, Dec. 30, 1945, p. 1031.

edge lies in the prevention of war. No system of safeguards that can be devised will of itself provide an effective guarantee against production of atomic weapons by a nation bent on aggression. Nor can we ignore the possibility of the development of other weapons, or of new methods of warfare, which may constitute as great a threat to civilization as the military use of atomic energy.[3]

Through the historical approach I have outlined, we find ourselves here to test if man can produce, through his will and faith, the miracle of peace, just as he has, through science and skill, the miracle of the atom.

The United States proposes the creation of an International Atomic Development Authority, to which should be entrusted all phases of the development and use of atomic energy, starting with the raw material and including—

1. Managerial control or ownership of all atomic-energy activities potentially dangerous to world security.

2. Power to control, inspect, and license all other atomic activities.

3. The duty of fostering the beneficial uses of atomic energy.

4. Research and development responsibilities of an affirmative character intended to put the Authority in the forefront of atomic knowledge and thus to enable it to comprehend, and therefore to detect, misuse of atomic energy. To be effective, the Authority must itself be the world's leader in the field of atomic knowledge and development and thus supplement its legal authority with the great power inherent in possession of leadership in knowledge.

I offer this as a basis for beginning our discussion.

But I think the peoples we serve would not believe—and without faith nothing counts—that a treaty, merely outlawing possession or use of the atomic bomb, constitutes effective fulfilment of the instructions to this Commission. Previous failures have been recorded in trying the method of simple renuncia-

[3] *Ibid.*, Nov. 18, 1945, p. 781.

tion, unsupported by effective guaranties of security and armament limitation. No one would have faith in that approach alone.

Now, if ever, is the time to act for the common good. Public opinion supports a world movement toward security. If I read the signs aright, the peoples want a program not composed merely of pious thoughts but of enforceable sanctions—an international law with teeth in it.

We of this nation, desirous of helping to bring peace to the world and realizing the heavy obligations upon us arising from our possession of the means of producing the bomb and from the fact that it is part of our armament, are prepared to make our full contribution toward effective control of atomic energy.

When an adequate system for control of atomic energy, including the renunciation of the bomb as a weapon, has been agreed upon and put into effective operation and condign punishments set up for violations of the rules of control which are to be stigmatized as international crimes, we propose that—

1. Manufacture of atomic bombs shall stop;
2. Existing bombs shall be disposed of pursuant to the terms of the treaty; and
3. The Authority shall be in possession of full information as to the know-how for the production of atomic energy.

Let me repeat, so as to avoid misunderstanding: My country is ready to make its full contribution toward the end we seek, subject of course to our constitutional processes and to an adequate system of control becoming fully effective, as we finally work it out.

Now as to violations: In the agreement, penalties of as serious a nature as the nations may wish and as immediate and certain in their execution as possible should be fixed for—

1. Illegal possession or use of an atomic bomb;
2. Illegal possession, or separation, of atomic material suitable for use in an atomic bomb;
3. Seizure of any plant or other property belonging to or licensed by the Authority;

4. Wilful interference with the activities of the Authority;

5. Creation or operation of dangerous projects in a manner contrary to, or in the absence of, a license granted by the international control body.

It would be a deception, to which I am unwilling to lend myself, were I not to say to you and to our peoples that the matter of punishment lies at the very heart of our present security system. It might as well be admitted, here and now, that the subject goes straight to the veto power contained in the Charter of the United Nations so far as it relates to the field of atomic energy. The Charter permits penalization only by concurrence of each of the five great powers—the Union of Soviet Socialist Republics, the United Kingdom, China, France, and the United States.

I want to make very plain that I am concerned here with the veto power only as it affects this particular problem. There must be no veto to protect those who violate their solemn agreements not to develop or use atomic energy for destructive purposes.

The bomb does not wait upon debate. To delay may be to die. The time between violation and preventive action or punishment would be all too short for extended discussion as to the course to be followed.

As matters now stand several years may be necessary for another country to produce a bomb, *de novo*. However, once the basic information is generally known, and the Authority has established producing plants for peaceful purposes in the several countries, an illegal seizure of such a plant might permit a malevolent nation to produce a bomb in 12 months, and if preceded by secret preparation and necessary facilities perhaps even in a much shorter time. The time required—the advance warning given of the possible use of a bomb—can only be generally estimated but obviously will depend upon many factors, including the success with which the Authority has been able to introduce elements of safety in the design of its plants and the degree to which illegal and secret preparation for the military use of atomic energy will have been eliminated. Presumably no nation would think of starting a war with only one bomb.

This shows how imperative speed is in detecting and penalizing violations.

The process of prevention and penalization—a problem of profound statecraft—is, as I read it, implicit in the Moscow statement, signed by the Union of Soviet Socialist Republics, the United States, and the United Kingdom a few months ago.

But before a country is ready to relinquish any winning weapons it must have more than words to reassure it. It must have a guarantee of safety, not only against the offenders in the atomic area but against the illegal users of other weapons— bacteriological, biological, gas—perhaps—why not?—against war itself.

In the elimination of war lies our solution, for only then will nations cease to compete with one another in the production and use of dread "secret" weapons which are evaluated solely by their capacity to kill. This devilish program takes us back not merely to the Dark Ages but from cosmos to chaos. If we succeed in finding a suitable way to control atomic weapons, it is reasonable to hope that we may also preclude the use of other weapons adaptable to mass destruction. When a man learns to say "A" he can, if he chooses, learn the rest of the alphabet too.

Let this be anchored in our minds:

Peace is never long preserved by weight of metal or by an armament race. Peace can be made tranquil and secure only by understanding and agreement fortified by sanctions. We must embrace international cooperation or international disintegration.

Science has taught us how to put the atom to work. But to make it work for good instead of for evil lies in the domain dealing with the principles of human duty. We are now facing a problem more of ethics than of physics.

The solution will require apparent sacrifice in pride and in position, but better pain as the price of peace than death as the price of war.

I now submit the following measures as representing the

fundamental features of a plan which would give effect to certain of the conclusions which I have epitomized.

1. General. The Authority should set up a thorough plan for control of the field of atomic energy, through various forms of ownership, dominion, licenses, operation, inspection, research, and management by competent personnel. After this is provided for, there should be as little interference as may be with the economic plans and the present private, corporate, and state relationships in the several countries involved.

2. Raw Materials. The Authority should have as one of its earliest purposes to obtain and maintain complete and accurate information on world supplies of uranium and thorium and to bring them under its dominion. The precise pattern of control for various types of deposits of such materials will have to depend upon the geological, mining, refining, and economic facts involved in different situations.

The Authority should conduct continuous surveys so that it will have the most complete knowledge of the world geology of uranium and thorium. Only after all current information on world sources of uranium and thorium is known to us all can equitable plans be made for their production, refining, and distribution.

3. Primary Production Plants. The Authority should exercise complete managerial control of the production of fissionable materials. This means that it should control and operate all plants producing fissionable materials in dangerous quantities and must own and control the product of these plants.

4. Atomic Explosives. The Authority should be given sole and exclusive right to conduct research in the field of atomic explosives. Research activities in the field of atomic explosives are essential in order that the Authority may keep in the forefront of knowledge in the field of atomic energy and fulfil the objective of preventing illicit manufacture of bombs. Only by maintaining its position as the best-informed agency will the Authority be able to determine the line between intrinsically dangerous and non-dangerous activities.

141

5. Strategic Distribution of Activities and Materials. The activities entrusted exclusively to the Authority because they are intrinsically dangerous to security should be distributed throughout the world. Similarly, stockpiles of raw materials and fissionable materials should not be centralized.

6. Non-Dangerous Activities. A function of the Authority should be promotion of the peacetime benefits of atomic energy.

Atomic research (except in explosives), the use of research reactors, the production of radioactive tracers by means of non-dangerous reactors, the use of such tracers, and to some extent the production of power should be open to nations and their citizens under reasonable licensing arrangements from the Authority. Denatured materials, whose use we know also requires suitable safeguards, should be furnished for such purposes by the Authority under lease or other arrangement. Denaturing seems to have been overestimated by the public as a safety measure.

7. Definition of Dangerous and Non-Dangerous Activities. Although a reasonable dividing line can be drawn between dangerous and non-dangerous activities, it is not hard and fast. Provision should, therefore, be made to assure constant re-examination of the questions and to permit revision of the dividing line as changing conditions and new discoveries may require.

8. Operations of Dangerous Activities. Any plant dealing with uranium or thorium after it once reaches the potential of dangerous use must be not only subject to the most rigorous and competent inspection by the Authority, but its actual operation shall be under the management, supervision, and control of the Authority.

9. Inspection. By assigning intrinsically dangerous activities exclusively to the Authority, the difficulties of inspection are reduced. If the Authority is the only agency which may lawfully conduct dangerous activities, then visible operation by others than the Authority will constitute an unambiguous danger signal. Inspection will also occur in connection with the licensing functions of the Authority.

U. S. Atom Bomb Proposals

10. Freedom of Access. Adequate ingress and egress for all qualified representatives of the Authority must be assured. Many of the inspection activities of the Authority should grow out of, and be incidental to, its other functions. Important measures of inspection will be associated with the tight control of raw materials, for this is a keystone of the plan. The continuing activities of prospecting, survey, and research in relation to raw materials will be designed not only to serve the affirmative development functions of the Authority but also to assure that no surreptitious operations are conducted in the raw-materials field by nations or their citizens.

11. Personnel. The personnel of the Authority should be recruited on a basis of proven competence but also so far as possible on an international basis.

12. Progress by Stages. A primary step in the creation of the system of control is the setting forth, in comprehensive terms, of the functions, responsibilities, powers, and limitations of the Authority. Once a charter for the Authority has been adopted, the Authority and the system of control for which it will be responsible will require time to become fully organized and effective. The plan of control will, therefore, have to come into effect in successive stages. These should be specifically fixed in the charter or means should be otherwise set forth in the charter for transitions from one stage to another, as contemplated in the resolution of the United Nations Assembly which created this Commission.

13. Disclosures. In the deliberations of the United Nations Commission on Atomic Energy, the United States is prepared to make available the information essential to a reasonable understanding of the proposals which it advocates. Further disclosures must be dependent, in the interests of all, upon the effective ratification of the treaty. When the Authority is actually created, the United States will join the other nations in making available the further information essential to that organization for the performance of its functions. As the successive stages of international control are reached, the United States will be prepared to yield, to the extent required by each stage, national control of activities in this field to the Authority.

143

14. International Control. There will be questions about the extent of control to be allowed to national bodies, when the Authority is established. Purely national authorities for control and development of atomic energy should to the extent necessary for the effective operation of the Authority be subordinate to it. This is neither an endorsement nor a disapproval of the creation of national authorities. The Commission should evolve a clear demarcation of the scope of duties and responsibilities of such national authorities.

And now I end. I have submitted an outline for present discussion. Our consideration will be broadened by the criticism of the United States proposals and by the plans of the other nations, which, it is to be hoped, will be submitted at their early convenience. I and my associates of the United States Delegation will make available to each member of this body books and pamphlets, including the Acheson-Lilienthal report, recently made by the United States Department of State, and the McMahon Committee Monograph No. 1 entitled "Essential Information on Atomic Energy" relating to the McMahon bill recently passed by the United States Senate, which may prove of value in assessing the situation.[4]

All of us are consecrated to making an end of gloom and hopelessness. It will not be an easy job. The way is long and thorny, but supremely worth traveling. All of us want to stand erect, with our faces to the sun, instead of being forced to burrow into the earth, like rats.

The pattern of salvation must be worked out by all for all.

The light at the end of the tunnel is dim, but our path seems to grow brighter as we actually begin our journey. We cannot yet light the way to the end. However, we hope the suggestions of my Government will be illuminating.

Let us keep in mind the exhortation of Abraham Lincoln, whose words, uttered at a moment of shattering national peril,

[4] Department of State publication 2498; for excerpts from the Acheson-Lilienthal report see *Department of State Bulletin*, Apr. 7, 1946, p. 553. The text of the McMahon bill is S. Rept. 1211, 79th Cong.

form a complete text for our deliberation. I quote, paraphrasing slightly:

> We cannot escape history. We of this meeting will be remembered in spite of ourselves. No personal significance or insignificance can spare one or another of us. The fiery trial through which we are passing will light us down in honor or dishonor to the latest generation.
>
> We say we are for Peace. The world will not forget that we say this. We know how to save Peace. The world knows that we do. We, even we here, hold the power and have the responsibility.
>
> We shall nobly save, or meanly lose, the last, best hope of earth. The way is plain, peaceful, generous, just—a way which, if followed, the world will forever applaud.

My thanks for your attention.

APPENDIX B

Toward Effective International Atomic Energy Control

STATEMENT BY U. S. REPRESENTATIVE BERNARD M. BARUCH
TO ATOMIC ENERGY COMMISSION, DECEMBER 5, 1946

My Fellow Members of the Atomic Energy Commission:

The primary responsibility for originating a system to protect the world against the atomic bomb has been placed squarely in our hands. Regardless of discussions elsewhere, the Atomic Energy Commission cannot escape its duty. Our task came to us from three high sources—first, the meeting in Washington, November a year ago, of the chiefs of state of the United States, Canada, and the United Kingdom; second, the meeting of the foreign ministers of the United States, the United Kingdom, and the Soviet Union, in Moscow last December; third, the definitive resolution of the General Assembly in London last January.

I note that the debates on disarmament in the General Assembly have followed closely the proposals laid down by the United States on June 14 before this body. It remains, however, the responsibility of this Commission to submit definite plans to the Security Council. It is to that business I address

146

myself. I entreat all to join in the enterprise so that we may show speed, as well as vision, in our assignment.

The stakes are greater than ever before offered mankind—peace and security. For who can doubt, if we succeed in controlling the atomic weapon, that we can go on to the control of other instruments of mass destruction? The elimination of war itself is within the range of possibility. I repeat: "The man who learns to say 'A' can learn, if he chooses, the rest of the alphabet, too."

But we must make a beginning. Let us delay no longer. The awakened conscience of humanity is our goal. In all my life, now past the biblical allotment of three score and ten years, never before have I seen so rich an opportunity for deathless service as is presented to us here. I want my country associated with victory in this great crusade.

For myself, as I look upon a long past and too short a future, I believe the finest epitaph would be—"He helped to bring lasting peace to the world."

But we must have whole-hearted and not halfway measures. The world is not to be fooled by lip service. The world will resent and reject deception. We must march together in the bonds of a high resolve. We dare not wait too long.

I do not intend, at this time, to debate the plan that we are about to offer here, in broad outline. I shall content myself with comments as to the imperative necessity for speed.

I beg you to remember that to delay may be to die. I beg you to believe that the United States seeks no special advantage. I beg you to hold fast to the principle of seeking the good of all, and not the advantage of one.

We believe that the original proposals of the United States, made on June 14th, were generous and just. Through the acid test of deliberation and debate, before this Commission and before the public opinion of the world, they have been proven so. In the long and protracted series of 70-odd meetings of this Commission and its various committees, studying all phases of the subject, we have found inherent and inevitable in any treaty that is to be written, covering this subject, three major elements:

1. The erection of an international authority which shall effectively prevent the manufacture and use of atomic bombs for war purposes, and which shall develop the use of atomic energy for social gain.

2. The right of free and full international inspection in support of these purposes.

3. The definite agreement that once a treaty becomes effective, providing for deterrents against offenses and punishments for offenders, there can be no veto to protect wilful violators, or to hamper the operations of the international authority.

However much one may seek to escape from these primaries, always the discussion, no matter where held, has come back to them. We have heard words that sometimes seemed to be steering us away from our goal, only later to hear others that led us back toward it.

The outline here presented is the bone and the sinew of any effective international control that may be—that shall be— *that must be established* if the civilized world is not to be ended; if the peoples are to live in security instead of being paralyzed by fear.

Time is two-edged. It not only forces us nearer to our doom, if we do not save ourselves, but, even more horrendous, it habituates us to existing conditions which, by familiarity, seem less and less threatening.

Once our minds have been conditioned to that sort of thinking, the keen edge of danger is blunted, and we are no longer able to see the dark chasm on the brink of which we stand.

Action at this time may well change hope to confidence. How can it profit any of us to avoid the issue, unless by so doing, we seek a special advantage; unless a chaos of fear will help particular ambitions?

Let us assume a report of the nature described in the American proposals is placed before the Security Council, together with such additions thereto as this body may desire. In it there will not be found a derogation of the dignity or might of any nation. On the contrary, the plan will build up, in all the world, a new and greater strength and dignity based on the faith that at last security is in sight; that at last men can walk erect again, no longer bent over by the numbing fear the atom bomb strikes into their hearts.

The price we have set upon the surrender of the absolute weapon is a declaration of peaceful intent and of interdependence among the nations of the world, expressed in terms of faith and given strength by sanctions—punishments to be meted out by concerted action against wilful offenders. That is one of the great principles of the United Nations—justice for all, supported by force. But there can be no unilateral disarmament by which America gives up the bomb, to no result except our own weakening. That shall never be.

It is for us to accept, or to reject—if we dare, this doctrine of salvation. It springs from stark necessity, and that is inexorable. My country, first to lay down a plan of cooperative control, welcomes the support of those countries which have already indicated their affirmative positions. We hope for the adherence of all.

We seek especially the participation of the Soviet Union. We welcome the recent authoritative statements of its highest representatives. From these, we are justified in concluding that it no longer regards the original American proposals unacceptable, as a whole or in their separate parts, as its member of this body stated at an earlier meeting.

I repeat—we welcome cooperation but we stand upon our basic principles even if we stand alone. We shall not be satisfied with pious protestations lulling the peoples into a false sense of security. We aim at an effective plan of control and will not accept anything less.

The time for action is here. Each of us perceives clearly what must be done. We may differ as to detail. We are in accord as to purpose. To the achievement of that purpose, I present a program in the form of resolutions, which have been placed before you.

I do not ask you to discuss or vote on these proposals at this time. They are now presented for your study and consideration. But I do ask the Chairman to call a meeting of this Commission, as early as convenient, to debate, if necessary, and

149

to act upon the findings and recommendations contained in these resolutions, so that the position each nation takes on them may be recorded in this Commission's report which must be drafted by December 20, and presented to the Security Council by December 31.

I shall now read these resolutions.

PROPOSALS BY THE UNITED STATES REPRESENTATIVE FOR THE CONSIDERATION OF THE ATOMIC ENERGY COMMISSION OF CERTAIN ITEMS TO BE INCLUDED AMONG THE FINDINGS AND RECOMMENDATIONS IN THE FORTHCOMING REPORT OF THE COMMISSION TO THE SECURITY COUNCIL

Pursuant to the resolution of this Commission passed at its meeting held November 13, 1946, the Report of the Proceedings, Findings and Recommendations of this Commission to be submitted to the Security Council by December 31, 1946, consists of three parts:

PART I, a Summary of the Proceedings together with the Records of this Commission and of its Committees and Subcommittees;

PART II, certain Findings of this Commission based upon its deliberations to date; and

PART III, certain Recommendations of this Commission based upon its Findings to date;

RESOLVED, that Part II of said report shall contain, among others, the following Findings of the Commission:

PART II: FINDINGS

Based upon the proposals and information presented to the Commission, upon the hearings, proceedings and deliberations of the Commission to date, and upon the proceedings, discussions and reports of its several committees and subcommittees, all as set forth in Part I of this report, the Commission has made the following findings:

(1) That scientifically, technologically and practically it is feasible,

> (*a*) to extend among "all nations the exchange of basic scientific information on atomic energy for peaceful ends, [1]
>
> (*b*) to control "atomic energy to the extent necessary to ensure its use only for peaceful purposes,"
>
> (*c*) to accomplish "the elimination from national armaments of atomic weapons," and
>
> (*d*) to provide "effective safeguards by way of inspection and other means to protect complying states against the hazards of violations and evasions."

(2) That effective control of atomic energy depends upon effective control of the production and use of uranium, thorium and their fissionable derivatives. Appropriate mechanisms of control to prevent their unauthorized diversion or clandestine production and use, including inspection, accounting, supervision, licensing and management, must be applied through the various stages of the processes from the time these minerals are severed from the ground to the time they become fissionable materials and are used.

(3) That, whether the ultimate fissionable product be destined for peaceful or destructive uses, the productive processes are identical and inseparable up to a very advanced stage of manufacture. Thus, the control of atomic energy to ensure its use for peaceful purposes, the elimination of atomic weapons from national armaments, and the provisions of effective safeguards to protect complying states against the hazards of violations and evasions must be accomplished through a single uni-

---

[1] Quotations are from the Commission's Terms of Reference, as set forth in article V of the Resolution providing for this Commission, passed by the General Assembly on Jan. 24, 1946.

fied international system of control designed to carry out all of these related purposes.

(4) That the development and use of atomic energy are not essentially and exclusively matters of domestic concern of the individual nations, but rather have predominantly international implications and repercussions.

(5) That an effective system of control of atomic energy must be international in scope, and must be established by an enforceable multilateral agreement (herein called "the treaty") which in turn must be administered by an international agency within the United Nations, possessing adequate powers and properly organized, staffed, and equipped for the purpose.

Only by such a system of international control can the development and use of atomic energy be freed from nationalistic rivalries with consequent risks to the safety of all peoples. Only by such a system can the benefits of widespread exchange of scientific knowledge and of the peaceful uses of atomic energy be assured. Only such a system of control would merit and enjoy the confidence of the people of all nations.

(6) That an international agreement outlawing the production, possession and use of atomic weapons is an essential part of any such system of international control of atomic energy. An international convention to this effect, if standing alone, would fail (*a*) "to ensure" the use of atomic energy "only for peaceful purposes" and (*b*) to provide for "effective safeguards by way of inspection and other means to protect complying states against the hazards of violations and evasions," and thus would fail to meet the requirements of the terms of reference of the Commission. To be effective, such an agreement must be an integral part of a treaty providing for a comprehensive system of international control and must be fortified by adequate guarantees and safeguards in the form of international supervision, inspection and control adequate to ensure the carrying out of the terms of the convention and "to protect complying states against the hazards of violations and evasions."

FURTHER RESOLVED, that Part III of said report shall contain, among others, the following recommendations:

International Control

Based upon the Findings of the Commission set forth in Part II of this report, the Commission makes the following Recommendations to the Security Council with respect to the matters covered by the Terms of Reference of the Commission, which recommendations are interdependent and not severable, constituting together and as a whole, the fundamental principles and basic organizational mechanisms necessary to attain the objectives set forth in the Commission's Terms of Reference.

(1) There should be a strong and comprehensive international system of control of atomic energy aimed at attaining the objectives set forth in the Commission's Terms of Reference.

(2) Such a system of international control of atomic energy should be established and its scope and functions defined by a treaty in which all of the nations members of the United Nations should be entitled to participate with the same rights and obligations. The international control system should be declared operative only when those members of the United Nations necessary to assure its success, by signing and ratifying the treaty, bind themselves to accept and support it.

(3) The treaty should include, among others, provisions

(a) Establishing, in the United Nations, an international authority (hereinafter called "the Authority") possessing powers and charged with responsibility necessary and appropriate for effective administration of the terms of the treaty, and for the prompt carrying out of its day-to-day duties. Its rights, powers, and responsibilities, as well as its relation to the several organs of the United Nations, should be clearly established and defined by the treaty. Such powers should be sufficiently broad and flexible to enable the authority to deal with new developments that may hereafter arise in the field of atomic energy. In particular, the authority shall be responsible for extending among all nations the exchange of basic scientific information on

153

atomic energy for peaceful ends, for preventing the use of atomic energy for destructive purposes and for stimulating its peaceful beneficent uses for the benefit of the people of all nations.

The Authority should have positive research and developmental responsibilities in order to remain in the forefront of atomic knowledge so as to render the Authority more effective in promoting the beneficent uses of atomic energy and in eliminating its destructive ones. The exclusive right to carry on atomic research for destructive purposes should be vested in the Authority.

Decisions of the authority pursuant to the powers conferred upon it by the treaty should govern the operations of national agencies for the control of atomic energy. In carrying out its prescribed functions, however, the Authority should interfere as little as necessary with the operations of national agencies for the control of atomic energy, or with the economic plans and the private, corporate and state relationships in the several countries.

(*b*) Affording the duly accredited representatives of the Authority unimpeded rights of ingress, egress and access for the performance of their inspections and other duties into, from and within the territory of every participating nation, unhindered by national or local authorities.

(*c*) Prohibiting the manufacture, possession, and use of atomic weapons by all nations parties thereto and by all of their nationals.

(*d*) Providing for disposal of any existing stocks of atomic bombs.

(*e*) Specifying the means and methods of determining violations of its terms, stigmatizing such violations as international crimes, and establishing the nature of the measures of enforcement and punishment to be imposed upon individuals and upon nations guilty of violating its provisions.

The judicial or other processes for determination of violations of the treaty and of punishment therefor, should be swift and certain. Serious violations of the treaty should be reported immediately by the Authority to the nations party to the treaty and to the Security Council. In dealing with such violations, the permanent members of the Security Council should agree not to exercise their power of veto to protect a violator of the terms of the treaty from the consequences of his wrongdoing.

The provisions of the treaty would be wholly ineffectual if, in any such situations, the enforcement provisions of the treaty could be rendered nugatory by the veto of a state which has voluntarily signed the treaty.

(4) The treaty should embrace the entire program for putting the system of international control of atomic energy into effect and should provide a schedule for the completion of the transitional process over a period of time, step by step in an orderly and agreed sequence leading to the full and effective establishment of international control of atomic energy. In order that the transition may be accomplished as rapidly as possible and with safety and equity to all, this Commission should supervise the transitional process, as prescribed in the treaty, and should be empowered to determine when a particular stage or stages have been completed and subsequent ones are to commence.

BIBLIOGRAPHY

Anonymous, *Mirrors of Wall Street*, G. P. Putnam's Sons, 1933.

Barton, Bruce, "Bernard Baruch Discusses the Future of American Business," *The American Magazine*, June, 1929.

Baruch, Bernard M., "Digging Out," *Saturday Evening Post*, May 1, 1920; "Some Aspects of the Farmer's Problems," *The Atlantic Monthly*, July, 1921; "Popular Fallacies About Reparations," *World's Work*, July, 1922; "Taking the Profit Out of War," *The Atlantic Monthly*, January, 1926; "A Few Kind Words for Uncle Sam," *Saturday Evening Post*, April 5, 1930; "The Dangers of Inflation," *Saturday Evening Post*, November 25, 1933; "Be Prepared!", *Review of Reviews*, April, 1937; "The Standards We Raise," *Survey Graphic*, November, 1941; "What of Our Future?", *Saturday Evening Post*, April 23, 1949.

Bent, Silas, "Three City-Bred Jews That the Farmer Trusts," *The Outlook*, August 8, 1923.

Coughlan, Robert, "Bernard Baruch," *Life*, January 10, 1944.

Creel, George, "Elevated to the Bench," *Collier's*, November 21, 1942.

Field, Carter, *Bernard Baruch: Park Bench Statesman*, Whittlesey House, McGraw-Hill Book Company, 1944.

Fortune, the editors of, "No Climax," October, 1933.

Gilbert, Clinton, *Mirrors of Washington*, G. P. Putnam's Sons, 1921.

Hersey, John, "The Old Man," *The New Yorker*, January 3, 10, and 17, 1948.

Hill, Edwin C., "Bernard M. Baruch," *Munsey's Magazine*, September, 1917.

Johnson, Alvin, "B.M.B., Prince of Israel," *Yale Review*, Spring, 1945.

Johnson, Hugh S., *The Blue Eagle from Egg to Earth*, Doubleday, Doran & Company, 1935.

Krock, Arthur, "Ulysses Ashore," *The New Yorker*, August 7, 1926.

Leigh, Virginia, "The Private Life of Bernard Baruch," *Collier's*, November 27, 1948.

Pegler, Westbrook, syndicated newspaper columns, October 31 and November 1, 1948.

Price, T. H., "Bernard Baruch: A Personal Portrait," *The Outlook*, May 8, 1918.

Shumway, H. I., *Bernard M. Baruch*, L. C. Page & Co., 1946.

Smith, Beverly, "Pinch Hitter for Presidents," *The American Magazine*, October, 1933.

Sullivan, Mark, "Bernard M. Baruch," *Collier's*, January 31, 1920.

Thomas, Henry and Dana Lee, *Fifty Great Americans*, Doubleday & Co., 1948.

Al